17 50 MN
01

BURT FRANKLIN: BIBLIOGRAPHY & REFERENCE SERIES 473
Philosophy and Religious History Monographs 122

A List of Editions of the Bay Psalm Book with a Facsimile Reprint of The First Edition

A List of Editions of the
ᗷAY ᑭSALM ᗷOOK

or

New England Version of the Psalms
Compiled by Wilberforce Eames

New Edition With

A Facsimile Reprint of the First
Edition of the Bay Psalm Book

Printed by Stephen Daye at Cambridge
In New England in 1640

BURT FRANKLIN
New York, N. Y.

Published by LENOX HILL Pub. & Dist. Co. (Burt Franklin)
235 East 44th St., New York, N.Y. 10017
Reprinted: 1973
Printed in the U.S.A.

Burt Franklin: Bibliography and Reference Series 473
Philosophy and Religious History Monographs 122

Library of Congress Cataloging in Publication Data

Eames, Wilberforce, 1855-1937.
  A list of editions of the Bay Psalm book or New England version of
the Psalms. Bound with a facsimile reprint of the 1640 ed. of the Bay
Psalm book.

  Eames' List is a reprint of the 1885 ed.
  1. Bible. O. T. Psalms. English—Paraphrases—Bay Psalm book—Bibliography.
2. Bible. O. T. Psalms—Paraphrases, English. I. Bay Psalm book. 1973. II. Title.
Z7772.E1E12 1973   016.223'2   72-10939
ISBN 0-8337-0987-9

Contents

A List of Editions of the
ᛒAY ᛒPSALM ᛒBOOK

or

New England Version of the Psalms
Compiled by Wilberforce Eames

"The Bay Psalm Book"

————— ♦♦♦ —————

In the preparation of the following list of editions of the New England version of the Psalms, I am under special obligations to George H. Moore, LL.D., of the Lenox Library, J. Hammond Trumbull, LL.D., of Hartford, and the late Mr. John A. Lewis of Boston.

The / V Vhole / Booke of Psalmes / Faithfully / Translated into English / Metre. / Whereunto is prefixed a discourse de- / claring not only the lawfullnes, but also / the necessity of the heavenly Ordinance / of singing Scripture Psalmes in / the Churches of / God. / Coll. III. / Let the word of God dwell plenteously in / you, in all wisdome, teaching and exhort- / ing one another in Psalmes, Himnes, and / spirituall Songs, singing to the Lord with / grace in your hearts. / Iames v. / If any be afflicted, let him pray, and if / any be merry let him sing psalmes. / *Imprinted* / 1640 / Sm. 8vo.

Collation: Title, surrounded by an ornamental type border, verso blank; "The Preface," 7 leaves, verso of last one blank; "The Psalmes In Metre," 139 leaves, ending below "Finis" with "An admonition to the Reader" in 18 lines; "Faults escaped in printing," 13 lines on one page, verso blank. Signatures *, **, A-LI in fours, making 148 leaves in all.

The first book printed in the British American colonies—preceded only by a broadside sheet and Pierce's almanac—and the earliest specimen known to be extant of the typography of Stephen Day, the first printer at Cambridge in New England. It was called the "Bay Psalm Book" from Massachusetts Bay, and was afterwards known as the "New England Psalm Book." The work of translation from the original Hebrew was commenced in 1636, and was the joint production of "the chief divines in the country," including, perhaps, some contributions from Francis Quarles, the poet; but the chief care in its production was confided to the Rev. Thomas Welde, the Rev. John Eliot, and the Rev. Richard Mather, the latter of whom wrote the long preface, which closes with the following words: "Neither let any think, that for the meetre sake wee have taken liberty or poeticall licence to depart from the true and proper sence of Davids words in the hebrew verses, noe; but it hath beene one part of our religious care and faithfull indeavour, to keepe close to the originall text. ... wee have therefore done our indeavour to make a plaine and familiar translation of the psalmes and words of David into english metre, and have not soe much as presumed to paraphrase to give the sense of his meaning in other words; we have therefore attended heerin as our chief guide the originall, shuning all additions, except such as even the best translators of them in prose supply, avoiding all materiall detractions from words or sence. ... If therefore the verses are not always so smooth and elegant as some may desire or expect; let them consider that Gods Altar needs not our polishings: Ex. 20. for wee have respected rather a plaine translation, then to smooth our verses with the sweetnes of any paraphrase, and soe have attended Conscience rather then Elegance, fidelity rather then poetry, in translating the hebrew words into english language, and Davids poetry into english meetre; that soe wee may sing in Sion the Lords songs of prayse according to his owne will; untill hee take us from hence, and wipe away all our teares, & bid us enter into our masters ioye to sing eternall Halleluiahs." "An admonition to the Reader," at the end of the volume, states that "The verses of these psalmes may be reduced to six kindes, the first whereof may be sung in very neer fourty common tunes; as they are collected, out of our chief musicians, by Tho. Ravenscroft."

The following portion of the 137th Psalm will serve as a specimen:

> The rivers on of Babilon
> there when wee did sit downe:
> yea, even then wee mourned, when
> we remembred Sion.
> Our Harps wee did hang it amid,
> upon the willow tree.
> Because there they that us away
> led in captivitee,
>
> Requir'd of us a song, & thus
> Askt mirth: us waste who laid,
> sing us among a Sions song,
> unto us then they said.
> The lords song sing can wee? being
> in strangers land Then let
> loose her skill my right hand, if I
> Ierusalem forget.

According to Thomas, the type used was Roman, of the size of small bodied English, entirely new. The punctuation is very bad, monosyllables being often divided at the ends of lines by hyphens, and polysyllables divided without them, and there are many typographical errors. For some unknown reason, the heading at the top of every left-hand page is printed "PSALM," while on every right-hand page is spelled and spaced "P S A L M E." A few words in Hebrew letters, which appear in the preface, may have been cut for the occasion on wood or on metal, as they evidently do not belong to any regular font of Hebrew type. Nine copies of this remarkable book are known to be extant, five of which were at one time in the "New England Library" of the Rev. Thomas

10

Prince. They are distributed as follows: (1) The Bodleian Library at Oxford, brqueathed with Bishop Tanner's books in 1735; (2) the Lenox Library, bought at the sale of the residue of Mr. Pickering's books at Sotheby's, Jan. 12th, 1855 (in lot 531); (3) the John Carter Brown Library, originally Richard Mather's copy, afterwards in the Prince Library, and sold at Dr. Shurtleff's sale in 1876, to C. Fiske Harris for $1,025; (4) Cornelius Vanderbilt of New York, from the Prince Library, and successively in the possession of Edward A. Crowninshield, Henry Stevens, and George Brinley, at whose sale, in 1897, it brought $1,200; (5) Mrs. George Livermore of Cambridge, Mass., from the Prince Library; (6) the American Antiquarian Society, at Worcester, lacking title-page and last leaf; (7 and 8) the Prince collection in the Boston Public Library, two copies, both slightly imperfect; (9) Harvard College Library, at Cambridge, Mass., lacking the first six and the last three leaves.

A Literal Reprint of the Bay Psalm Book Being the Earliest New England Version of the Psalms and the First Book Printed in America (Fifty Copies for Subscribers) *Cambridge Printed for Charles B. Richardson New York* 1862 8vo, pp. vii; Reprint of the Psalms, (148) leaves; List of Subscribers, pp. (2). A., B.

Edited by Dr. Nathaniel B. Shurtleff. Fifty copies printed on common paper for subscribers, fifteen copies on thick paper, five copies on India paper, and one copy on parchment.
"In the reproduction of this quaint volume every word, every letter, and indeed every point has been sedulously collated with a perfect impression of the original work struck at Cambridge in the year 1640. ... Indeed, so exact and faithful has the compositor been in following the original copy, that the bad spacing, omission of spaces, irregular justification, bad division, broken type, letters inverted, mixed lower-case letters with italics, and typographical errors, are strictly reproductions of the printers' errors of the olden time."—*Preface*

The / Whole Book / of / Psalmes, / Faithfully translated into / English Metre: / Whereunto is prefixed a discourse, declaring not / onely the lawfulnesse, but also the necessity / of the heavenly Ordinance of sing- / ing Scripture Psalmes in the / Churches of God. / Col. 3. 16. / Let the word of God dwell plenteously in you, / in all wisdome, teaching and exhorting one ano- / ther in Psalmes, Hymns, and spirituall Songs, / singing to the Lord with grace in your hearts. / James 5. 13. / If any be afflicted, let him pray; and if any be / merry, let him sing Psalmes. / *Imprinted* 1647. / Sm. 12mo.   BM., J.C.B.

11

Collation: Title, verso blank; "The Preface" in six leaves; the Psalms, pp. 1-274. Sig. A—M in twelves.

This is a mere reprint of the first edition, including the preface, and "An admonition to the Reader" on page 274. It is in smaller type, and much better printed than the edition of 1640, with some changes and corrections in the spelling and punctuation. It may have been printed at Cambridge, N.E., by Stephen Day—perhaps by Matthew Day—but some experts have supposed that it was really printed in England. Only two copies are known to be extant, one of which was sold at Mr. Brinley's sale, in 1879, for $435. *See* "Notes and Queries," 2nd Series, ix. 218-219; and "Historical Magazine," iv, 310; x, 18.

The / Psalms / Hymns And Spiritual / Songs / Of the Old and New Test- / ament, faithfully translated / into English metre, / For the use, edification, and comfort, / of the Saints, in publick, & private. / especially in New-England. / 2 Tim: 3. 16, 17. / Col. 3. 16. Let the word of God dwell in / you richly in all wisdom, teaching & ad- / monishing one another in Psalms, Hymns, / and spirituall / Songs, singing to the Lord / with grace in your hearts. / Ephe: 5. 18, 19. Bee filled with &c: / James 5. 13. / *Printed by Samuel Green at Cambridg / in New-England.* 1651. / Sm. 8vo. (4 1/16 x 2 1/2 inches.)

Collation: Title, verso blank; To the Godly Reader, 2 leaves; The Song of Moses, The Song of Deborah and Barak, The Song of Hannah, and Davids Elegie, 9 leaves, verso of last one blank; The Book of Psalms, pp. 1-314; The Song of Songs which is Solomons, The Songs in the Prophet Isaiah, The Lamentations of Jeremiah, The Prayer of Jonah, A Prayer of Habakkuk, The Song of the blessed virgine Mary, The Song of Zacharias, and Songs from Revelations, etc., 21 leaves; Errata of 15 lines on one page, verso blank. Sig. ** and *₊* in ones, A—Y in eights, and Z in four, not including the title-page.

This is a new edition, revised and improved by the Rev. Henry Dunster, President of Harvard College, and Mr. Richard Lyon. It is the first to contain the Spiritual Songs, which were added by Mr. Lyon. The only copy I know of is in the unrivalled collection of Mr. C. H. Kalbfleisch of New York. It is in the original binding and in perfect condition. Thomas ("History of Printing") mentions a similar title, "crown 8 vo, 308 pages," but puts it under the year 1650.

The Psalmes Hymns and Spiritual Songs of the Old and New Testament, faithfully Translated into English Metre. For the Use, Edification and Comfort of the Saints in Publick and Private, especially in New-England. With a Preface concerning the Duty of Singing Psalms. *London:*

12

Printed for John Blague. 1652. 12mo.

This title is given on the authority of Kennett's "Bibliothecae Americanae Primordia."

The / Psalms, / Hymns, / and / Spiritual Songs / of the / Old and New Testament, / Faithfully Translated into / English Metre. / For the use, edification and comfort of the / Saints in publick and private, espe- / cially in New-England. / 2 Tim. 3: 16, 17. / Col. 3: 16. Let the word of God dwell in you richly in / all wisdome, teaching and admonishing one another / in Psalms, Hymns, and Spirituall Songs, singing to / the Lord with grace in your hearts. / Ephes. 5: 18. 19. Be filled with, &cc./ James 5: 13. / *Cambridge, / Printed for Hezekiah Usher, of Bostoo [sic]. [1658?]* 12mo.

Collation: 7 prel. leaves, containing title, verso blank, The Preface in 5 pages, To the Godly Reader on 1 page, passages from the Old Testament versified on 1 page, and The Song of Moses, The Song of Deborah and Barak, The Song of Hannah, and Davids Elegie in 5 pages; The Book of Psalms, pp. 1-93; The Song of Songs which is Solomons, The Songs in the prophet Isaiah, The Lamentations of Jeremiah, The Prayer of Jonah, A Prayer of Habakkuk, The Song of the blessed Virgin Mary, The Song of Zacharias, and Songs from Revelations, etc., pp. 94-106, ending on page 106 with "Finis." In double columns, with 60 lines in a full column. Sig. A—I in sixes, and K in five, not including the title-page.

Probably printed at Cambridge in England. The name of Hezekiah Usher, a prominent merchant and bookseller in Boston, appears in the imprints of several books from 1650 to 1664, and that of his son John Usher from 1669 to 1696 or later. The type used in this and the two following editions is a well shaped nonpareil letter, which does not appear in any work known to have been printed in this country at that time. Dr. J.H. Trumbull writes: "Mr. Usher went to England in the autumn of 1657, charged with matters of business for the Commissioners of the United Colonies. Not improbably, this edition of the Psalms was printed, or contracted for, when he was in London." Mr. Haven ("Ante-Revolutionary Catalogue," p. 8,) says: "It is possible that Mr. Usher ordered copies printed at Cambridge in England to be bound up with the small Bibles printed there and elsewhere for the New England market. Other copies with the same imprint, varying slightly in size, and with some changes in the spelling of words in the text are met with. ... Mr. Thomas's copy [of the following edition] was bound with a Bible printed at Cambridge, England, by Roger Daniel, 1648. The Psalms are similarly associated with Bibles printed in other places and of other dates." The only copy of this edition that I know of was sold at the Brinley sale for

$90, and is now in the library of Brown University at Providence.

The / Psalms, / Hymns, / and / Spiritual Songs / of the / Old and New Testament, / Faithfully Translated into / English Metre. / For the use, edification and comfort of the / Saints in publick and private, espe- / cially in New-England. / 2 Tim. 3: 16, 17. / Col. 3: 16. Let the word of God dwell in you richly in / all wisdome, teaching and admonishing one another / in Psalms, Hymns, and Spiritual Songs, singing to / the Lord with grace in your hearts. / Ephes. 5: 18, 19. Be filled with, &c. / James 5: 13. / *Cambridge, / Printed for Hezekiah Usher, of Bostoò [sic]. / [1665?]* 12mo.   L.

Collation: Title, verso blank; The Preface, pp. 3-6; To the Godly Reader, p. 7; passages from the Old Testament versified, pp. 7-8; The Song of Moses, The Song of Deborah and Barak, The Song of Hannah, and Davids Elegie, pp. 8-12; The Book of Psalms, pp. 12-90; The Song of Songs which is Solomons, Songs from Isaiah, Lamentations, Jonah, Habakkuk, etc., pp. 90-100, ending on page 100 with "Finis." In double columns, with 65 lines in a full column. Sig. A—H in sizes, and I in two.

This edition also was probably printed in England. The copy described above is bound with a small Bible with the imprint: *Printed / By Roger Daniel, Printer to / The Universite of / Cambridge / 1648. /* Another copy in the Lenox Library, which lacks all after page 94, but is otherwise in fine condition, was purchased at the sale of Mr. E.B. Corwin's books in New York in 1856 (No. 2445), and afterwards catalogued by Mr. Henry Stevens ("Nuggets," No. 2256) at 10 ICS. The copy in the library of the American Antiquarian Society at Worcester lacks portions of pages 91-94, and all after, and has the last word in the imprint correctly spelled *Boston*. It contains the following manuscript note on a fly leaf; "N.B. This copy was originally bound up with a Bible printed in England, from which I took it. I suppose this was printed in 1665, and in this form to bind up with small Bibles printed in England for New England.—I. Thomas." Mr. Thomas, who supposed from the imprint that it was printed in this country, gives the following account of the book: "This was, I believe the third edition of the New England Version of the Psalms after it had been revised and improved by president Dunster, &c., and the fifth, including all the former editions. I have a complete copy of this edition [with 100 pages], but the name of the printer, and the year in which it was printed, are not mentioned. It is calculated by being printed in a small page, with a very small type, to bind up with English editions of the pocket Bible; and, as the printing is executed by a good workman, and is the best that I have seen from the Cambridge press, I conclude, therefore, it could not be printed by Green before the arrival of Marmaduke Johnson in 1660; I have no doubt it was printed under Johnson's care; and, probably, soon after the Indian Bible came from the press in 1663. ... Although in
14

this edition the typography far exceeds in neatness any other work then printed in the country, it is very incorrect; but this might have been more the fault of the corrector of the press, than of the printer. My belief that it was published about the year 1664, or 1665, is confirmed by its being printed for Hezekiah Usher, the only bookseller that I can find an account of at that time in New England. ... It is a curious fact, that nonpareil types were used so early in this country; I have not seen them in any other book printed either at Cambridge, or Boston, before the revolution; even brevier types had been but seldom used in the printing houses in Boston earlier than 1760. The nonpareil used for the Psalms was new, and a very handsome faced letter."—*History of Printing,* second edition, I. 69.

The / Psalms, / Hymns, / and Spiritual Songs / of the / Old and New Testament, / Faithfully Translated into / English Metre. / For the use, edification and comfort of the Saints / in publick and private, especially in / New-England. / 2 Tim. 3: 16. 17. / Col. 3: 16. Let the word of God dwell in you richly in all wis- / dome, teaching and admonishing one another in Psalms, / Hymns, and Spiritual Songs, singing to the Lord with grace / in your hearts. / Ephes. 5: 18. 19. Be filled with, &c. / James 5: 13. / *Cambridge, / Printed for Hezekiah Usher, of Boston.* / *[*n. d.*]* 12mo.   B.

Collation: Title, verso blank; The Preface, pp. 3-5; To the Godly Reader, followed by passages from the Old Testament versified, p. 6; The Song of Moses, etc., pp. 7-10; The Book of Psalms, pp. 10-76; The Song of Songs which is Solomons, Songs from Isaiah, Lamentations, Jonah, Habakkuk, etc., pp. 76-84, ending on page 84 with "Finis." In double columns, with 72 lines in a full column. Sig. A—G in sixes.

I am indebted to the late Mr. John A. Lewis, of Boston, for the following account of this edition: "The work here described is bound with Canne's Bible, which Bible is without place or printer's name, but is dated 1682. Of Canne's Bible, Timperley (page 531) says: 'an edition was on sale in England at the com- mencement of the nineteenth [eighteenth?] century dated 1682, with a London title, though printed at Amsterdam.' The Psalm Book is an exceedingly fine piece of work, and was (as it appears to me) bound up *originally* with the Bible. I call the type non- pareil, and am tolerably certain the work was not printed at Cam- bridge in Old England. It may have been printed in Holland." Loftie ("Century of Bibles," No. 374) says of Canne's Bible: "No place or printer's name.) 1682. 12mo. With Canne's notes. Probably printed in Holland, but sometimes attributed to the Edinburgh press. Very incorrect," etc.

The / Psalms, / Hymns, / and / Spiritual Songs, / of the / Old & New Testament, / Faithfully Translated into / English Meeter. / For the Use, Edification and Com- / fort

15

of the Saints in publick and private, / especially in New-England. / ... / The Fifth Edition. / *London, Printed by A.C. for Ric. Chiswel, / at the Two Angels and Crown in / Little Britain.* 1671. / Sm. 12mo. (4 1/2 x 2 inches.)   L.

The / Psalms, / Hymns, / and / Spiritual Songs / Of the / Old & New Testament, / faithfully translated into / English Meeter. / For the use, edification and comfort of / the Saints in publick and private, / especially in New-England. / ... / The Fifth Edition. / *London: Printed for Richard Chiswell / at the Rose and Crown in St. Pauls / Church-Yard.* 1680. / Sm. 12mo, pp. (36), 304, (43).   B.

The Psalms, Hymns, and Spiritual Songs, of the Old and New Testament, faithfully translated into English Meeter, for the Use, edification and Comfort of the Saints in Publick and private, especially in New-England. *London: Printed for R. Chiswell.* 1694. Sm. 12mo.

The / Psalms, / Hymns, / and / Spiritual Songs / of the / Old and New Testament, / faithfully translated into / English Meeter. / For the Use, Edification and Comfort of / the Saints in publick and private, es- / pecially in New-England. / ... / London; / *Printed for S.W. for the use of his Majesty's / Colony in New-England,* 1697. / 12mo.

16

pp. 1-84, and over?

The above title was furnished by Mr. George T. Little, of Bowdoin College Library, Brunswick, Maine, from a copy in that collection which lacks a portion of pp. 83-84, and all after.

The / Psalms / Hymns, / and / Spiritual Songs, / of the / Old & New-Testament: Faithfully / Translated into English Meetre. / For the Use, Edification and Com- / fort of the Saints in publick and / private, especially in New-England. / ... / The Ninth Edition. / *Boston, Printed by B. Green, and F. Allen, / for Michael Perry, under the West- / End of the Town house.* 1698. / Sm. 12mo.   M.

Collation: Title-page, with "To the Godly Reader" on verso; short verses, pp. 3-5; The Song of Moses, pp. 5-9; The Prophetical Song of Moses, pp. 9-16; The Song of Deborah and Barak. pp. 16-21; The Song of Hannah, pp. 21-22; Davids Elegy, pp. 22-24; Psalms, pp. 24-365; The Song of Songs which is Solomons, pp. 366-383; The Songs in the Prophet Isaiah, chap. V., XII., XXV., XXVI., XXXVIII., pp. 383-393; The Lamentations of Jeremiah, chap. III., V., pp. 393-400; The Prayer of Jonah, pp. 400-401; A Prayer of Habakkuk, pp. 401-404; The Song of the blessed Virgin Mary, pp. 404-405; The Song of Zacharias, pp. 405-406; The Song of Simeon, pp. 406-407; songs from Revelation (beginning with chap. IV., verse 8, and ending with chap. XIX., verse I), pp. 407-410; A Table for the whole Book of Psalms, pp. 411-418; The Tunes of the Psalms. Some few directions for ordering the Voice in Setting these following Tunes of the Psalms (*i.e.* Oxford Tune, Low Dutch Tune, York Tune, Windsor Tune, Cambridge Short Tune, St. Davids Tune, Martyrs Tune, Hackney Tune, Psalm 119 Second Meeter, Psalm 100 First Meeter, Psalm 115 First Meeter, and Psalm 148 First Meeter), pp. 419-(430). Sig. A-R in twelves, and S in eleven.

The "tunes" are cut on wood. At the end of this copy is bound a sort of appendix, lacking the first leaf, and containing from the middle of the ninth verse to the end of the twenty-first verse of another metrical version of the twenty-sixth chapter of Isaiah, First Meeter, pp. 3-5; Isaiah XXVI., Second Meeter Usual, pp. 6-9; The Doxology, of the Angels, In Luke II. 14, p. 10. Concerning this appendix, I have received the following note from Dr. Moore of the Lenox Library:

"I have found notices of two editions of the Bay Psalm Book not included in your list. Cotton Mather has left the record in his own hand that on the '2^d 3^m [1699] There is printing a New Edition of the Psalm Book. In every former edition that excellent portion of Scripture, the 26th chapter of Isaiah was in such a metre, that few of or Churches could sing. Whereupon I this day, took a few minutes to turn it into another metre, with perhaps a smoother and sweeter version. So 'tis published in the psalm book and tho this were but a small action, yett I felt a Great Comfort when I thought, that the praises of God would bee the more sung, throughout this Wilderness, for any of my poor Endeavours.' I have not met with this edition, but in the Lenox copy of the Boston

17

edition of 1706, which you have described, pp. 360-369 contain an 'Appendix. Some Essays to fit that Excellent portion of Prophetick Scripture, in the Twenty-sixth Chapter of Isaiah, unto the Tunes more commonly used in our Psalmody.' Two versions are given of the chapter, one the 'First Meeter. 8 & 8,' the other 'Second Meeter, Usual.' These are followed by 'A Specimen taken out of a New Version of the Psalms of David, Composed by Nich. Brady, and Nahum Tate'—being the Psalms LXXXII, and CXXXVII. An advertisement in Clough's Almanac for 1706 states that 'There is now in Press and may speedily be published a New Edition of the *New England Psalm Book:* Printed with a New Fair Character, and on good fine Paper: with a New Sett of most Common Tunes more free from Errors than heretofore.' [The second edition of Boone's Military Discipline is mentioned also, and] 'These two Printed for and Sold by *Benjamin Eliot* at his Shop under the West End of the Town-House in Boston, and *Nicholas Boone* at his Shop near School House Lane.' "

The Psalm Book last referred to is probably the same as the following edition with a different imprint:

The / Psalms / Hymns, / and / Spiritual Songs, / of the / Old and New-Testament: Faith- / fully Translated into / English Meeter. / For the Use, Edification and Comfort / of the Saints in Publick and Private, / especially in New-England. / ... / The Thirteenth Edition. / *Boston: Printed by B. Green, for / Nicholas Buttolph, at his Shop at the / Corner of Gutteridg's Coffee-House.* 1706. / Sm. 12mo.

Collation: Title-page, with "To the Godly Reader" on verso; short verses, pp. 3-5; The Song of Moses, pp. 5-8; The Propheticall Song of Moses, pp. 8-14; The Song of Deborah and Barak, pp. 14-18; The Song of Hannah, pp. 19-20; Davids Elegy, pp. 20-21; Psalms, pp. 22-319; The Song of Songs which is Solomons, pp. 320-335; The Songs in the Prophet Isaiah, chap. V., XII., XXV., XXVI., XXXVIII., pp. 335-344; The Lamentations of Jeremiah, chap. III., V., pp. 344-350; The Prayer of Jonah, pp. 350-351; A Prayer of Habakkuk, pp. 351-353; The Song of the blessed Virgin Mary, pp. 353-354; The Song of Zecharias, pp. 354-355; The Song of Simeon, p. 356; songs from Revelation (beginning with chap. IV., verse 8, and ending with chap. XIX., verse I), pp. 356-359; The Doxology of the Angels. In Luke, chap. II., verse 14, p. 359; Appendix. Some Essays to fit that Excellent portion of Prophetick Scripture, in the Twenty sixth Chapter of Isaiah, unto the Tunes more commonly used in our Psalmody. First Meeter. 8 & 8. Isaiah XXVI., pp. 360-364; Isaiah XXVI. Second Meeter, Usual, pp. 364-367; A Specimen taken out of a New Version of the Psalms of David, Composed by Nich. Brady, and Nahum Tate—Psalm LXXXII., pp. 367-368; Psalm CXXXVII., pp. 368-369; A Table for the whole Book of Psalms, pp. 370-376; The Tunes of the Psalms. Some few Directions, etc. (with tunes engraved on wood), pp. 377-[384?] Sig. A—Q in twelves. In the Lenox Library.

The copy described above lacks about two leaves at the end. Some copies of this edition have the imprint: *Boston: Printed by*

18

B. Green, for Samuel Phillips at the Brick Shop. 1706. *See also* the note to the edition of 1698, *supra.* Frequently reprinted as follows:

The Tenth Edition. *London.* 1706. Sm. 12mo.

The Fourteenth Edition. *Boston: Printed by John Allen, for Eleazer Phillips, under the Exchange in Kings-street.* 1709. Sm. 12mo, pp. 340. 12 Tunes. M.

The Twelfth Edition. *London, Printed for Tho. Varnam and John Osborn, at the Oxford-Arms in Lombard-Street.* 1713. Sm. 12mo, pp. (7), 97. Sig. A-H in sixes, and I in four. L.

The Fifteenth Edition. *Boston: Printed by T. Crump, for S. Gerrish.* 1713. Small 12mo.

The Sixteenth Edition. *Boston: Printed by John Allen, for Eleazer Phillips, in Butler's Row, at the Lower-End of King-Street,* 1715. Sm. 12mo, pp. 378, (4). W.

The Seventeenth Edition. *Boston: Printed by B. Green, for Benjamin Eliot, and Sold at his Shop in King-Street.* 1716. 12mo. pp. 378. 12 Tunes. M.

The Eighteenth Edition. *Boston.* 1717. 12mo.

The Nineteenth Edition. *Boston: Printed by T. Crump, for S. Gerrish.* 1718. 12mo, pp. 376. 12 Tunes.

The Thirteenth Edition. *London, Printed for John Osborn, at the Oxford-Arms in Lombard-street.* 1719. Sm. 12mo, pp. (6), 90. Sig. A-H in sixes. L.

The Twentieth Edition. *Boston: Printed by F. Franklin, for D. Henchman at the corner Shop over against the Brick Church in Cornhill.* 1722. 12mo, pp. 312, including 11 Tunes. M.

The Fifteenth Edition. *London: Printed by J.H. for F. Osborn, and T. Longman at the Ship and Black-Swan in Pater-Noster-Row.* 1725. 12mo, pp. (12), 84. Sig. A-H in sixes. L. This edition contains the "Preface."

The Twenty-first Edition. *Boston.* 1726. 12mo.

The Twenty-second Edition. *Boston: Printed for J. Phillips at the Stationers Arms, next door to Mr. Polhiers near the Dock.* 1729. 12mo, pp. (2), 309, including 12 Tunes.

The Seventeenth Edition. *London, Printed for F. Osborn, and T. Longman, at the Ship in Pater-noster-row.* 1729. 12mo, pp. (6), 90.

The Twenty-third Edition. *Boston: Printed for D. Henchman over against the Brick Meeting-House in Cornhil.* 1730. 12mo. pp. (2), 346, including 12 Tunes. Sig. A-O in twelves, and P in six. L., M.

The Sixteenth Edition. *Edinburgh: Printed by Robert Free-bairn and Company, His Majesty's Printers.* MDCCXXXII. 12mo. pp. (8), 44 and over. H.

The Twenty-fourth Edition. *Boston, N.E. Printed by S. Knee-land & T. Green, for the Booksellers.* 1737. 12mo, pp. (2), 346, including 12 Tunes. S., W.

The Seventeenth Edition. *London: Printed by J.H. for I. Long-man, at the Ship in Pater Noster Row.* 1737. 12mo.

The Eighteenth Edition. *London: Printed for F. Osborn and T. Longman, at the Ship in Pater-noster-row.* 1741. 12mo, pp. (6), 90.

The Eighteenth Edition. *Edinburgh.* 1741. 12mo.

The Twenty-fifth Edition. *Printed for Daniel Henchman and Thomas Hancock, in Boston.* 1742. 12mo, pp. (2), 346.   M.

The Twenty sixth Edition. *Boston, N.E. Printed by F. Draper, for M. Dennis near Scarlet's Wharff.* 1744. 12mo, pp. (2), 346   H.

The Eighteenth Edition. *London: T. and T. Longman.* M. DCC. LIV. 12mo, pp. (6), 90.

Edinburgh, 1754. 12mo.

The Twenty-second Edition. *Edinburgh: Printed by Alexander Kincaid, Printer to His Majesty.* 1759. 12mo.

The Twenty-seventh Edition. *Boston: Printed and Sold by Tho-mas and John Fleet, at the Heart & Crown in Cornhill.* 1762. 12mo, pp. 334.   W.

The portions contributed by Cotton Mather in 1699 were re-printed in the later Boston editions, in some of which all the "songs" were placed *after* the Psalms. The London editions are in double columns, in a very small type, and generally without the "Preface." After 1762, this version was superseded by "The New-England Psalter," and Brady and Tate's "New Version of the Psalms."

20

Facsimile Reprint of the
First Edition Printed
In 1640

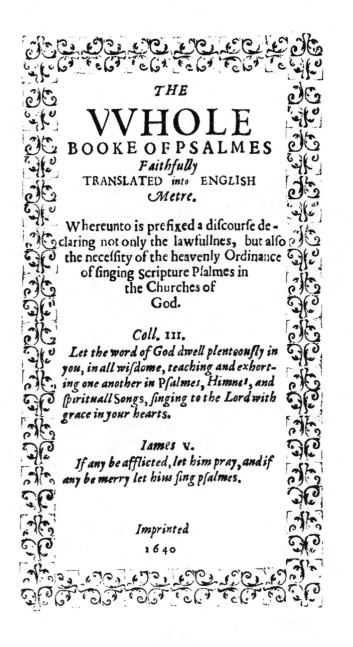

THE
VVHOLE
BOOKE OF PSALMES
Faithfully
TRANSLATED *into* ENGLISH
Metre.

Whereunto is prefixed a difcourfe declaring not only the lawfullnes, but alfo
the neceffity of the heavenly Ordinance
of finging Scripture Pfalmes in
the Churches of
God.

Coll. III.
*Let the word of God dwell plenteoufly in
you, in all wifdome, teaching and exhorting one another in Pfalmes, Himnes, and
fpirituall Songs, finging to the Lord with
grace in your hearts.*

Iames V.
*If any be afflicted, let him pray, and if
any be merry let hiw fing pfalmes.*

Imprinted
1640

The Preface.

THe singing of Pfalmes, though it breath forth nothing but holy harmony, and melody : yet fuch is the fubtilty of the enemie, and the enmity of our nature againft the Lord, & his wayes, that our hearts can finde matter of difcord in this harmony, and crotchets of divifion in this holy melody .-for- There have been three queftiõs efpecially ftirrĩg cõcerning finging. Firft.what pfalmes are to be fung in churches? whether Davids and cther fcripture pfalmes, or the pfalmes invented by the gifts of godly men in every age of the church. Secondly, if fcripture pfalmes, whether in their owne words, or in fuch meter as englifh poetry is wont to run in? Thirdly· by whom are they to be fung? whether by the whole churches together with their voices? or by one man finging alõe and the reft joynĩg in filéce,& in the clofe fayĩg amen.

Touching the firft, certainly the finging of Davids pfalmes was an acceptable worfhip of God, not only in his owne, but in fucceeding times. as in Solomons time 2 *Chron.* 5.13. in Iehofaphats time 2 *chron.* 20. 2r. in Ezra his time *Ezra* 3. 10,11. and the text is evident in Hezekiahs time they are commanded to fing praife in the words of David and Afaph, 2 *chron.* 29, 30. which one place may ferve to refolve two of the queftions (the firft and the laft) at once. for this commandement was it ceri-

moniall

moniall or morall ? some things in it indeed were
cerimoniall, as their musicall inftruments &c
but what cerimony was there in singing prayse
with the words of David and Asaph ? what if David was a type of Christ, was Asaph also ? was
every thing of David typicall ? are his words
(which are of morall, universall, and perpetuall
authority in all nations and ages) are they typicall ? what type can be imagined in making use
of his songs to prayse the Lord ? If they were typicall becaufe the cerimony of musicall inftruments was joyned with them, then their prayers
were also typicall, becaufe they had that ceremo-
ny of incenfe admixt with them : but wee know
that prayer then was a morall duty, notwithftand-
ing the incenfe; and foe singing those pfalmes not-
withftanding their musicall inftruments. Befide,
that which was typicall (as that they were sung
with musicall inftruments, by the twenty-foure
orders of Priefts and Levites. 1 *chron* 2 5. 9.) muft
have the morall and spirituall accomplifhment in
the new Teftament, in all the Churches of the
Saints principally, who are made kings & priefts
Reu. 1. 6. and are the firft fruits unto God. *Reu*.14
4. as the Levites were *Num*. 3. 45. with hearts &
lippes, in ftead of musicall inftruments, to prayse
the Lord; who are fet forth (as fome iudicioufly
thinke) *Reu*.4. 4. by twéty foure Elders, in the ripe
age of the Church, *Gal*.4. 1, 2, 3. anfwering to the
twenty foure orders of Priefts and Levites
1 *chron*. 25. 9. Therefore not fome felect
members

members, but the whole Church is commaunded to teach one another in all the severall sorts of Davids psalmes, some being called by himselfe מִזְמוֹרִים : psalms, some תְּהִלִּים : Hymns some שִׁירִים : spirituall songs. soe that if the singing Davids psalmes be a morall duty & therfore perpetuall; then wee under the new Testamēt are bound to sing them as well as they under the old: and if wee are expresly commanded to sing Psalmes, Hymnes, and spirituall songs, then either wee must sing Davids psalmes, or else may affirm they are not spirituall songs: which being penned by an extraordiary gift of the Spirit, for the sake especially of Gods spirituall Israell; not to be read and preached only (as other parts of holy writ) but to be sung also, they are therefore most spirituall, and still to be sung of all the Israell of God: and verily as their sin is exceeding great, who will allow Davids psalmes (as other scriptures) to be read in churches (which is one end) but not to be preached also,(which is another end soe their sin is crying before God, who will allow them to be read and preached, but seeke to deprive the Lord of the glory of the third end of them, which is to sing them in christian churches.
obj. 1 If it be sayd that the Saints in the primitive Church did compile spirituall songs of their owne inditing, and sing them before the Church. 1Cor. 14, 15, 16.
Ans. We answer first, that those Saints compiled these spirituall songs by the extraordinary gifts of

* 3   the

the spirit (common in those dayes) whereby they were inabled to praise the Lord in strange tongues, wherin learned *Pareus* proves those psalmes were uttered, in his Commēt on that place *uers* 14 which extraordinary gifts, if they were still in the Churches, wee should allow them the like liberty now. Secondly, suppose those psalmes were sung by an ordinary gift (which wee suppose cannot be evicted) doth it therefore follow that they did not, & that we ought not to sing Davids psalmes? must the ordinary gifts of a private man quench the spirit still speaking to us by the extraordinary gifts of his servant David? there is not the least foot-step of example, or precept, or colour reason for such a bold practise.

obj. 2. Ministers are allowed to pray conceived prayers, and why not to sing conceived psalmes? must wee not sing in the spirit as well as pray in the spirit?

Ans. First because every good minister hath not a gift of spirituall poetry to compose extemporary psalmes as he hath of prayer. Secondly. Suppose he had, yet seeing psalmes are to be sung by a joynt consent and harmony of all the Church in heart and voyce (as wee shall prove) this cannot be done except he that composeth a psalme, bringeth into the Church set formes of psalmes of his owne invētion; for which wee finde no warrant or president in any ordinary officers of the Church throughout the sciptures. Thirdly. Because the booke of psalmes is so compleat a System of

psalmes

pſalmes, which the Holy-Ghoſt himſelfe in infinite wiſdome hath made to ſuit all the conditions,
neceſſityes, temptations, affections, &c. of men
in all ages; (as moſt of all our interpreters on the
pſalmes have fully and perticularly cleared)there
fore by this the Lord ſeemeth to ſtoppe all mens
mouths and mindes ordinarily to compile or
ſing any other pſalmes (under colour that the
ocaſions and conditions of the Church are new)
&c. for the publick uſe of the Church, ſeing, let
our condition be what it will, the Lord himſelfe
hath ſupplyed us with farre better; and therefore
in Hezekiahs time, though doubtleſſe there were
among them thoſe which had extraoridnary gifts
to compile new ſongs on thoſe new ocaſions, as
Iſaiah and Micah &c. yet wee read that they are
commanded to ſing in the words of David and
Aſaph, which were ordinarily to be uſed in the
publick worſhip of God: and wee doubt not but
thoſe that are wiſe will eaſily ſee; that thoſe
ſet formes of pſalmes of Gods owne appoynt-
ment not of mans conceived gift or humane
impoſition were ſung in the Spirit by thoſe holy Levites, as well as their prayers were in
the ſpirit which themſelves conceived, the
Lord not then binding them therin to any
ſet formes ; and ſhall ſet formes of pſalmes
appoynted of God not be ſung in the ſpirit now,
which others did then ?

Queſton. But why may not one compoſe a pſalme
& ſing it alone with a loud voice & the reſt joyne
with

with him in silence and in the end say **Amen?**

Ans. If such a practise was found in the **Church**
of **Corinth,** when any had a psalme suggested by
an extraordinary gift; yet in singing ordinary
psalmes the whole Church is to ioyne together
in heart and voyce to prayse the Lord. -for-

First. Davids psalmes as hath beene shewed,
were sung in heart and voyce together by the
twenty foure orders of the musicians of the Tem
ple, who typed out the twenty foure Elders all
the members especially of christian Churches *Rev*
5. 8. who are made Kings and Priests to God
to prayse him as they did : for if there were
any other order of singing Choristers beside
the body of the people to succeed those, the
Lord would doubtlesse have given direction
in the gospell for their quallification, election,
maintainance &c. as he did for the musicians of
the Temple, and as his faithfullnes hath done for
all other church officers in the new Testament.

Secondly. Others beside the Levites (the chiefe
Singers) in the Iewish Church did also sing the
Lords songs; else why are they commanded frequently to sing: as in pf. 100, 1, 2, 3. pf. 95, 1, 2, 3.
pf. 102. title. with vers 18. & *Ex.* 15. 1. not only
Moses but all Israell sang that song, they spake
saying (as it is in the *orig.*) all as well as Moses,
the women also as well as the men. v. 20 21. and
deut. 32. (whereto some thinke, Iohn had reference as well as to *Ex.* 15. 1. when he brings in the
protestant Churches getting the victory over the
Beast

Beaſt with harps in their hands and ſinging the ſong of Moſes. *Reu.* 15. 3.) this ſong Moſes is commanded not only to put it into their hearts but into their mouths alſo: *deut.* 31. 19. which argues, they were with their mouths to ſing it together as well as with their hearts.

Thirdly. Iſaiah foretells in the dayes of the new-Teſtament that Gods watchmen and deſolate loſt ſoules, (ſignified by waſt places) ſhould with their voices ſing together, Iſa. 52. 8, 9. and *Reu.* 7. 9, 10. the ſong of the Lamb was by many together, and the Apoſtle expreſly commands the ſinging of Pſalmes, Himnes, &c. not to any ſelect chriſtians, but to the whole Church Eph. 5. 19 *coll.* 3. 16. Paule & Silas ſang together in private *Acts.* 16. 25. and muſt the publick heare ōly one man ſing? to all theſe wee may adde the practiſe of the primitive Churches; the teſtimony of ancient and holy *Baſil* is in ſtead of many *Epiſt.* 63 When one of us (ſaith he) hath begun a pſalme, the reſt of us ſet in to ſing with him, all of us with one heart and one voyce; and this ſaith he is the common practiſe of the Churches in Egypt, Lybia, Thebes, Paleſtina, Syria and thoſe that dwell on Euphrates, and generally every where, where ſinging of pſalmes is of any account. To the ſame putpoſe alſo *Euſebius* gives witnes, *Eccleſ. Hiſt. lib.* 2. *cap.* 17. The objections made againſt this doe moſt of them plead againſt joyning to ſing in heart as well as in voyce, as that by this meanes others out of the Church will ſing

** as

as also that wee are not alway in a sutable estate
to the matter sung, & likewise that all cannot sing
with understanding ; shall not therefore all that
have understanding ioyne in heart and voyce to -
gether ? are not all the creatures in heaven, earth,
seas : men, beasts, fishes, foules &c. commanded
to praise the Lord, and yet none of these but
men, and godly men too , can doe it with
spirituall understanding ?

As for the scruple that some take at the trans-
latiō of the book of psalmes into meeter, because
Davids psalmes were sung in his owne words
without meeter : wee answer- First. There are
many verses together in several psalmes of David
which run in rithmes (as those that know the hebrew and as Buxtorf shews *Thesau.* pa. 629.) which
shews at least the lawfullnes of singing psalmes in
english rithmes .

Secondly. The psalmes are penned in such
verses as are sutable to the poetry of the hebrew
language, and not in the common style of such
other bookes of the old Testament as are not
poeticall ; now no protestant doubteth but that
all the bookes of the scripture should by Gods
ordinance be extant in the mother tongue of each
nation, that they may be understood of all, hence
the psalmes are to be translated into our english tongue; and if in our english tongue wee are
to sing them, then as all our english songs (accord
ing to the course of our english poetry) do run in
metre, soe ought Davids psalmes to be translated
into

into meeter, that foe wee may fing the Lords
fongs, as in our engliſh tongue foe in fuch verſes
as are familar to an engliſh eare which are commonly metricall: and as it can be no juſt offence
to any good confcience to fing Davids hebrew
fongs in engliſh words, foe neither to firg his
poeticall verſes in engliſh poeticall metre: men
might as well ſtumble at firging the hebrew
pſalmes in our engliſh tunes (and not in the hebrew tunes) as at finging them in engliſh meeter,
(which are our verſes) and not in fuch verſes as
are generally uſed by David according to the poetry of the hebrew language: but the truth is, as
the Lord hath hid from us the hebrew tunes, leſt
wee ſhould think our felves bound to imitate
them; foe alfo the courſe and frame (for the moſt
part) of their hebrew poetry, that wee might not
think our felves bound to imitate that, but that
every nation without fcruple might follow as the
graver fort of tunes of their owne country fongs,
foe the graver fort of verſes of their owne country poetry.

Neither let any think, that for the meetre
fake wee have taken liberty or poeticall licence
to depart from the true and proper fence of
Davids words in the hebrew verſes, noe; but it
hath beene one part of our religious care and
faithfull indeavour, to keepe cloſe to the
originall text.

As for other obiections taken from the diffi-
culty of *Ainſworths* tunes, and the corruptions in

✳ ✳ 2   our

our common pfalme books, wee hope they are
anfwered in this new edition of pfalmes which
wee here prefent to God and his Churches. For
although wee have caufe to bleffe God in many
refpects for the religious indeavours of the
tranflaters of the pfalmes into meetre ufually an-
nexed to our Bibles, yet it is not unknowne to
the godly learned that they have rather prefented
a paraphrafe then the words of David tranflated according to the rule *2 chron.* 29. 30. and
that their addition to the words, detractions from
the words are not feldome and rare, but very fre-
quent and many times needles, (which we fup-
pofe would not be approved of if the pfalmes
were fo tranflated into profe) and that their
variations of the fenfe, and alterations of the
facred text too frequently, may iuftly minifter
matter of offence to them that are able to com -
pare the tranflation with the text; of which fail-
ings, fome iudicious have oft complained,
others have been grieved, wherupon it hath bin
generally defired, that as wee doe inioye other,
foe (if it were the Lords will) wee might inioye
this ordinance alfo in its native purity: wee have
therefore done our indeavour to make a plaine
and familiar tranflation of the pfalmes and words
of David into englifh metre, and have not foe
much as prefumed to paraphrafe to give the fenfe
of his meaning in other words; we have therefore
attended heerin as our chief guide the originall,
fhunning all additions, except fuch as even the beft
                                        tranflators

tranllators of them in profe fupply, avoiding all materiall dettactions from words or fence. The word ץ which wee tranflate *and* as it is redundant fometime in the Hebrew, foe fomtime (though not very often) it hath been left out, and yet not then, if the fence were not faire without it.

As for our tranflations, wee have with our englifh Bibles (to which next to the Originall wee have had refpect) ufed the Idioms of our owne tongue in ftead of Hebraifmes, left they might feeme englifh barbarifmes.
Synonimaes wee ufe indifferently: as *folk* for *people*, and *Lord* for *Iehovah*, and fomtime (though feldome) *God* for *Iehovah*; for which (as for fome other interpretations of places cited in the new Teftament) we have the fcriptures authority pf. 14. with 53. Heb. 1. 6. with pfalme 97. 7.
Where a phrafe is doubtfull wee have followed that which (in our owne apprehenfiō) is moft genuine & edifying:

Somtime wee have contracted, fomtime dilated the fame hebrew word, both for the fence and the verfe fake: which dilatation wee conceive to be no paraphrafticall addition no more then the contraction of a true and full tranflation to be any unfaithfull detraction or diminution: as when wee dilate *who healeth* and fay *he it is who healeth*; foe when wee contract, *thofe that ftand in awe of God* and fay *Gods fearers*.

Laftly. Becaufe fome hebrew words have a
** 3   more

more full and emphaticall signification then any one english word can or doth somtime expresse, hence wee have done that somtime which faithfull translators may doe, *viz.* not only to translate the word but the emphasis of it; as אל *mighty God*, for God. ברך *humbly blesse* for *blesse*; *rise to stand*, psalm 1. for *stand*; *truth and faithfullnes* for *truth*. Howbeit, for the verse sake wee doe not alway thus, yet wee render the word truly though not fully; as when wee somtime say *reioyce* for *shout for ioye*.

As for all other changes of numbers, tenses, and characters of speech, they are such as either the hebrew will unforcedly beare, or our english forceably calls for, or they no way change the sence; and such are printed usually in an other character.

If therefore the verses are not alwayes so smooth and elegant as some may desire or expect; let them consider that Gods Altar needs not our pollishings: Ex. 20. for wee have respected rather a plaine translation, then to smooth our verses with the sweetnes of any paraphrase, and foe have attended Conscience rather then Elegance, fidelity rather then poetry, in translating the hebrew words into english language, and Davids poetry into english meetre;
that

that foe wee may fing in Sion the Lords
fongs of prayfe according to his owne
will; untill hee take us from hence,
and wipe away all our teares , &
bid us enter into our mafters
ioye to fing eternall
Halleluiahs.

THE PSALMES

In Metre

PSALME I

O Blessed man, that in th'advice
  of wicked doeth not walk:
nor stand in sinners way, ror sit
  in chayre of scornfull folk.

2 But in the law of Iehovah,
  is his longing delight:
aud in his law doth meditate,
  by day and eke by night.

3 And he shall be like to a tree
  planted by water-rivers:
that in his season yeilds his fruit,
  and his leafe never withers.

4 And all he doth, shall prosper well,
  the wicked are not so:
but they are like vnto the chaffe,
  which winde drives to and fro.

5 Therefore shall not ungodly men,
  rise to stand in the doome,
nor shall the sinners with the iust,
  in their assemblie *come.*

6 For of the righteous men, the Lord
  acknowledgeth the way:
but the way of vngodly men,
  shall vtterly decay.

A   PSALM

PSALM II

VVHy rage the *Heathen* furiously?
     mule vaine things people do;
2 Kings of the earth doe set themselves,
     Princes consult also:
     with one consent against the Lord,
     and his anoynted one.
3 Let us asunder break their bands,
     their cords bee from us throwne.
4 Who sits in heav'n shall laugh; the lord
     will mock them; then will he
5 Speak to them in his ire, and wrath:
     and vex them suddenlie.
6 But I annoynted have my King
     upon my holy hill
7 of Zion: The established
     counsell declare I will.
  God spake to me, thou art my Son:
     this day I thee begot.
8 Aske thou of me, and I will give
     the Heathen for thy lot:
     and of the earth thou shalt possesse
     the utmost coasts abroad.
9 thou shalt them break as Potters sherds
     and crush with yron rod.
10 And now yee Kings be wise, be learn'd
     yee Iudges of th'earth(*Heare.*)
11 Serve yee the lord with reverence,
     rejoyce in him with feare.
12 Kisse yee the Sonne, lest he be wroth,
     and yee fall in the way.
  when his wrath quickly burnes, oh blest

                     are

are all that on him ftay .
Pfalme 3
1 A pfalme of David when he fled from the
face of Abfalom his Sonne.

O Lord, how many are my foes?
   how many up againft me ftand?
2 Many fay to my foule noe helpe
   in God for him at any hand.
3 But thou Lord art my fhield, my glory
   and the-uplifter of my head,
4 with voyce to God I cal'd, who from
   his holy hill me anfwered.
5 I layd me downe, I flept, I wakt,
   for Iehovah did me up beare:
6 People that fet againft me round,
   ten thoufand of them I'le not feare.
7 Arife o Lord, fave me my God,
   for all mine enimies thou haft ftroke
   upon the cheek-bone :& the teeth
   of the ungodly thou haft broke.
8 This, and all fuch falvation,
   belongeth vnto Iehovah;
   thy bleffing is, and let it be
   upon thine owne people. Selah.
Pfalme 4
To the cheife Mufician on *Neginoth,*
a pfalme of David.

G OD of my juftice, when I call
   anfwer me: when diftreft
thou haft inlarg'd me, fl ew me grace,
   and heare thou my requeft.

A 2   2 yee

PSALM IV

2 Ye Sonnes of men, my glory turne
    to shame how long will you?
how long will ye love vanity,
    and still deceit pursue?

3 But know, the Lord doth for himselfe
    set by his gracious saint :
the Lord will heare when I to him
    doe poure out my complaint.

4 Be stirred up, but doe not sinne,
    consider seriouslie:
within your heart upon your bed;
    and wholly silent be

5 Let sacrifices of justice,
    for sacrifices be,
and confidently put your trust
    on Iehovah doe ye.

6 Many there be that say o who,
    will cause us good to see:
the light, Lord, of thy countenance
    let on us lifted be.

7 Thou hast put gladnesse in my heart,
    more then the time wherein
their corne, and also their new wine,
    have much increased bin.

8 In peace with him I will lye downe,
    and take my sleepe will I:
For thou Lord mak'st me dwell alone
    in confident safety.

Psalme 5

1 To the cheife Musitian upon *Nehiloth*,
    a psalme of David.

psalm

PSALME V

Heare thou my words and understand
   my meditation, Iehovah.

2 My King, my God, attend the voyce
   of my cry: for to thee I pray.

3 At morn Iehovah, thou shalt heare
   my voyce: to thee I will addresse

4 at morn, I will looke up. For thou
   art not a God lov'st wickednesse
   neither shall evil with thee dwell.

5 Vaine glorious fooles before thine eyes
   shall never stand: for thou hatest
   all them that worke iniquities.

6 Thou wilt bring to distruction
   the speakers of lying-falshood,
   the lord will make to be abhor'd
   the man deceitfull, and of blood.

7 But I will come into thine house
   in multitude of thy mercy:
   and will in feare of thee bow downe,
   in temple of thy sanctity.

8 Lead me forth in thy rightousnes,
   because of mine observing spies,
   O Iehovah doe thou thy wayes
   make straight, and plaine, before mine eyes

9 For there no truth is in his mouth,
   their inward part iniquities;
   their throat an open sepulchre,
   their tongue is bent to flatteries.

10 O God make thou them desolate
   from their owne plots let them fall far,
   cast them out in their heapes of sinnes,

for they againſt thee Rebells are.

11 *An I* all that truſt in thee ſhall joy,
and ſhout for joy eternallie,
and thou ſh ilt them protect: & they
that love thy name ſhall joy in thee.

12 Forthou Iehovah, wilt beſtow
a bleſſing on the rightous one:
and wilt him crowne as with a ſheild,
with gracious acceptation.

Pſalme 6

To the chief Muſician on N*eginoth* upon-
Sheminith, a pſalme of David

LORD in thy wrath rebuke me not,
nor in thy hot wrath chaſten me·

2 Pitty me Lord, for I am weak,
Lord heale me, for my bones vext be.

3 Alſo my ſoule is troubled ſore:
how long Lord wilt thou me forſake?

4 Returne o Lord, my ſoule releaſe:
o ſave me for thy mercy ſake.

5 In death no mem'ry is of thee
and who ſh ill prayſe thee in the grave?

6 I faint with groanes, all night my bed
ſwims, I with tears my couch waſht have.

7 mine eye with grief is dimme and old:
becauſe of all mine enimies.

8 But now depart away fom me,
all yee that work iniquities:
for Iehovah ev'n now hath heard
the voyce of theſe my weeping teares.

9 Iehovah heare my humble ſuit,

Iehovah

Iehovah doth receive my prayers,
10 Let all mine enimies be asham'd
and greatly troubled let them be:
yea let them be returned back,
and be ashamed suddenlie.

Psalme 7

Shiggaion of David which he sãg to Iehovah
upõ the words of Cush the Ben,amite.

O LORD my God in thee
I doe my trust repose,
save and deliver me from all
my persecuting foes.
2 Left like a Lion hee
my soule in peeces teare:
rending asunder, while there is
not one deliverer.
3 Iehovah o my God
if this thing done have I :
if so there be within my hands
wrongfull iniquiry
4 If I required ill
the man with me at peace,
(yea I have him delivered
that was my foe causlesse:)
5 Let foe pursue my soule,
and take, and tread to clay
my life: and honor in the dust
there let him wholly lay
6 Arise Lord in thy wrath
for th'enimies fiercenesse:
be thou lift up, & wake to me,

A 4   judgemēt

judgement thou did'ſt expreſſe.

7 So thee encompaſſe round
   ſhall peoples aſſembly;
and for the ſame doe thou returne,
   vnto the place on high.

8 The Lord ſhall judge the folke;
   Iehovah judge thou me.
according to my righteouſneſſe,
   and mine integritie.

9 Let ill mens malice ceaſe,
   but doe the juſt couſirme,
for thou who art the righteous God:
   doſt hearts and reins diſcerne.

10 For God my ſheild, the right
   in heart he ſaved hath.

11 The God that doth the rightous judge,
   yet daily kindleth wrath.

12 If he doe not returne,
   his ſword he ſharp will whet:
his bow he bended hath, and he
   the ſame hath ready ſet.

13 For him he hath prepar'd
   the inſtruments of death,
for them that hotly perſecute,
   his arrows he ſharpneth.

14 Behold he travelleth
   of vaine iniquity:
a toyleſome miſcheife he conceiv'd,
   but ſhall bring forth a lye.

15 A pit he digged hath,
   and delved deepe the ſame:

but

But fall'n he is into the ditch,
    that he himselfe did frame.
16 His mischeivous labour
    shall on his head turn downe:
and his injurious violence
    shall fall upon his crowne.
17 Iehovah I will prayse
    for his just equity;
and I will sing unto the name
    of Iehovah most high.

Psalme 8

To the chiefe Musician upon *Gittith*,
    a psalme of David.

O LORD our God in all the earth
    how's thy name wondrous great:
who hast thy glorious majesty
    above the heavens set.
2 out of the mouth of sucking babes.
    thy strength thou didst ordeine,
that thou mightst still the enemy,
    and them that thee disdaine.
3 when I thy fingers work, thy Heav'ns,
    the moore and starres consider
4 which thou hast set. What's wretched man
    that thou dost him remember?
or what's the Son of man, that thus
    him visited thou hast?
5 For next to Angells, thou hast him
    a litle lower plac't
and hast with glory crowned him,
    and comely majesty:

B

6 and

6 And on thy works haſt given him,
    lordly authoriy.

7 All haſt thou put under his feet;
    all ſheep and oxen, yea

8 and beaſts of field. Foules of the ayre,
    and fiſhes of the ſea,
      and all that paſſe through paths of ſeas.

9 O Iehovah our Lord,
   how wondrouſly-magnificent
     is thy name through the world?

Pſalme 9

To the chiefe Muſician upon *Muth-Labben*
a pſalme of David

LORD I'le the prayſe, with all my heart;
   thy wonders all proclaime.

2 I will be glad and joy in thee;
   moſt high, I'le ſing thy name.

3 In turning back my foes, they'le fall
   and periſh at thy ſight.

4 For thou maintaines my right, & cauſe:
   In throne ſits judging right.

5 Thou t' heathen checkſt, & th'wicked ſtroyd;
   their names raz'd ever aye.

6 Thy ruines, foe, for aye are done;
   thou madſt their townes decaye;
their memory with them is loſt.

7 Yet ever ſits the Lord:
his throne to judgement he prepares.

8 With right he'l judge the world:
he to the folke ſhall miniſter
   judgement in uprightneſſe.

9 The Lord is for th'opreſt a ſort:
   a ſort in times of ſtreſſe.
10 Who knowes thy name, will truſt in thee;
   nor doſt thou, Lord forſake,
11 them that thee ſeek. Pſalmes, to the Lord
   that dwells in Sion, make:
   declare among the folk his works.
12 For blood when he doth ſeeke,
   he them remembers: nor forgets
   the crying of the meeke.
                  (2)
13 Iehovah, mercy on me have,
   from them that doe me hate
   marke mine afflictions that ariſe,
   thou lift'ſt me from deaths-gate.
14 That I may tell in the gates of
   the Daughter of Sion,
   thy prayſes all: and may rejoyce
   in thy ſalvation.
15 The heathen are ſunk downe into
   the pit that they had made:
   their owne foot taken is ith'net
   which privily they layd.
16 By judgement which he executes
   Iehovah is made knowne:
   the wicked's ſnar'd in's owne hand work.
   deepe meditation.
17 The wicked ſhall be turn'd to hell,
   all lands that God forget.
18 Forgot the needy ſhall ne're be:
   poores hope ne're faild him yet.

19 Arise,o Lord, left men prevaile,
    judge t⁶ heathen in thy fight.
20 That they may know they be but men,
    the nations Lord affright.   Selah

Pſalme 10

WHy ſtandſt thou Lord a far ? why hyd'ſt
    thy ſelfe in times of ſtreight?

2 In pride the wicked perſecutes
    the poore afflicted wight:
ſnare them in their contrived plots.

3 For of his hearts deſire
    the wicked boaſts, and covetous
    bleſſeth, ſtirring Gods ire.

4 The wicked one by reaſon of
    his countenances pride
will not ſeek *after God*: not God
    ſo all his thoughts abide.

5 his wayes doe alwayes bring forth griefe,
    on high thy judgements bee
above his fight: his preſſing foes
    puffe at them all will hee.

6 Within his heart he thus hath ſayd,
    I moved ſhall not bee:
fron aye to aye becauſe I *am*
    not in adverſitie.

7 His mouth with curſing filled *is*,
    deceits, and fallacy:
under his tongue perverſnes *is*,
    alſo iniquity.

8 In the cloſe places of the townes
    he ſits, in ſecret dens

he flays the harmleffe: 'gainft the poore
flyly his eyes downe bends.

9 He clofely lurks as lion lurks
in den, the poore to catch
he lurks, & trapping them in 's net
th' afflicted poore doth fnatch.

10 Downe doth he crowtch,& to the duft
humbly he bowes *with-all*:
that fo a multitude of poore
in his ftrong pawes may fall .

11 He faith in heart, God hath forgot:
he hides his face away,
fo that he will not fee this thing
unto eternall aye.

(2)

12 Iehovah rife thou up,o God
lift thou thine hand on hy,
let not the meek afflicted one
be out of memory.

13 Wherefore doth the ungodly man
contemne th' almighty one?
he in his heart faith, thou wilt not
make inquifition.

14 Thou feeft,for thou markft wrong,& fpight,
with thy hand to repay:
the poore leavs it to thee,thou art
of fatherleffe the ftay.

15 Break thou the arme of the wicked,
and of the evil one.
fearch thou out his impiety,
untill thou findeft none.

B 3   16 Iehov-

16 Iehovah king for ever is,
   and to eternall aye:
out of his land the heathen folke
   are perished away.
17 The meeke afflicted-mans desire
   Iehovah, thou dost heare:
thou firmly dost prepare their heart,
   thou makst attent thine eare.
18 To judge the fatherlesse & poore:
   that adde no more he may
sorrowfull man out of the land
   with terror to dismay.

Psalme 11

To the chiefe Musician a psalme
of David.

In the Lord do trust; how then
   to my soule doe ye say,
as doth a litle bird unto
   your mountaine flye away?
2 For loe, the wicked bend their bow,
   their arrows they prepare
on string; to shoot in dark at them
   in heart that upright are.
3 If that the firme foundationes,
   utterly ruin'd bee:
as for the man that righteous is,
   what then performe can hee?
4 The Lord in's holy temple is,
   the Lords throne in heaven:
his eyes will view, and his eye lids
   will prove the Sonnes of men.

5 the

5 The man that truly-righteous is
   ev'n him the Lord will prove;
his foule the wicked hates, & him
   that violence doth love.

6 Snares, fire, & brimftone he will raine,
   ungodly men upon:
and burning tempeft; of their cup
   fhall-be their portion.

7 For Iehovah that righteous is,
   all righteoufneffe doth love:
his countenane the upright one
   beholding, doth approve.

Pfalme 12

To the chiefe Mufician upon *Sheminith*
   a pfalme of David.

HElpe Lord: for godly men doe ceafe:
   faithfull faile men among.

2 Each to his freind fpeaks vanity;
   with flattring lips, *and tongue*
and with a double heart they fpeake.

3 All flatt'ring lips the Lord
   fhall cut them of, with every tongue
   that fpeaketh boafting word.

4 Thus have they fayd, we with our tongue,
   prevailing pow're fhall get:
are not our lips our owne. for Lord
   who over us is fet?

5 Thus faith the Lord, for fighs of them
   that want, for poor oppreft,
I'le now arife, from fuch as puffe,
   will fet him fafe at reft.

B 4   6 pure

PSALM XII, XIII.

6 Pure are the words the Lord doth speak:
      as silver that is tryde
   in earthen furnace, seven times
      that hath been purifyde.
7 Thou shalt them keep, o Lord, thou shalt
      preserve them ev'ry one,
   For evermore in safety from
      this generation.
8 The wicked men on evry side
      doe walk presumptuously,
   when as the vilest sons of men
      exalted are on hye.

Psalme 13
To the chiefe Musician: a psalme
of David.

O IEHOVAH, how long
      wilt thou forget me aye?
   how long wilt thou thy countenance
      hide from me farre away?
2 How long shall I counsell,
      in my soule take, sorrow
   in my heart dayly? o're me set
      how long shall be my foe?
3 Iehovah, o my God,
      behold me answer make,
   Illuminate mine eyes, lest I
      the sleepe of death doe take.
4 Lest my foe say, I have
      prevaild 'gainst him: & me
   those who doe trouble, doe rejoyce,
      when I shall moved bee.

5 But

5 But I afured truft
    have put in thy mercy;
my heart in thy falvation
    fhall joy exceedingly.
6 Vnto Iehovah I
    will fing, becaufe that hee,
for evil bountifully hath
    rewarded good to mee.

Pfalme 14
To the chiefe Mufician a pfalme
of Dauid.

THe foole in's heart faith ther's no **God**;
    they are corrupt, have done
abominable-practifes,
    that doth good there is none.
2 The Lord from heaven looked downe
    on Sonnes of men: to fee,
if any that doth underftand,
    that feeketh God there bee.
3 All are gone back, together they
    ev'n filthy are become:
and there is none that doeth good,
    noe not fo much as one.
4 The workers of iniquityes,
    have they no knowledge all?
that eate my people: they eate bread,
    and on God doe not call.
5 There with a very grievous feare
    affrighted fore they were,
for God in generation is
    of fuch as righteous are.

C   the

6 The counsell yee would make of him
    that poore afflicted is,
to be asham'd & that because
    the Lord his refuge is.
7 Who Israels health from Syon gives?
    his folks captivitie
when God shall turne: Iacob shall joye
    glad Israel shall be.
            Psalme 15
        A psalme of David.
IEHOVAH, who shall in thy tent
    so ourne, and who is hee
shall dwell within thy holy mount?
2 He that walks uprightlie,
    And worketh justice, and speaks truth
3 in s heart, And with his tongue
he doth not slander, neither doth
    unto his neighbour wrong,
    And 'gainst his neighbour that doth not
    take up reproachfull lyes.
4 Hee that an abject person is
    contemn'd is in his eyes;
But he will highly honour them
    that doe Iehovah feare:
and changeth not, though to his losse,
    if that he once doe sweare.
5 Nor gives his coyne to vsury,
    and bribe he doth not take
against the harmelesse. he that doth
    these things shall never shake.

                        PSALM

Psalme 16
Michtam of David
O Mighty God, preserve thou mee,
  for on thee dœ I rest.
2 Thou art my God, vnto the Lord
  my soule thou hast profest:
  My goodnes reacheth not to thee.
3 But to the Saints upon
    the earth & to the excellent,
    whome all my joye is on.
4 They who give gifts to a strange God,
    their sorrowes multiplye:
  their drink oblations of blood
    offer up will not I.
  Neither will I into my lips
    the names of them take up.
5 Iehovah is the portion
    of my part, & my cup:
  Thou art maintainer of my lot.
6 To me the lines fal'n bee
  in pleasant places:yea,faire is
    the heritage for mee.
7 I will Iehovah humbly-blesse,
    who hath mee counselled:
  yea in the nights my reines have mee,
    chastising nurtured.
8 Iehovah I have alwayes set
    as present before mee:
  because he is at my right hand
    I shall not moved bee.
9 Wherefore my heart rejoyced hath,
      C 2   and

and glad is my glory:
moreover also my flesh shall
in hope lodge securely.

10 Because thou wilt not leave my soule
within the grave to bee,
nor wilt thou give thine holy one,
corruption for to see.

11 Thou wilt shew me the path of life,
of joyes abundant-store
before thy face, at thy right hand
are pleasures evermore.

Psalme 17
A Prayer of David.

HArken, o Lord, unto the right,
attend vnto my crye,
give eare vnto my pray'r, that goes
from lips that doe not lye.

2 From thy face let my judgement come:
thine eyes the right let see.

3 Thou provst mine heart, thou visitest
by night, and tryest mee.
yet nothing find'st, I have resolvd
my mouth shall not offend.

4 From mens works: by word of thy lips
I spoylers paths attend.

5 Stay my feet in thy paths, lest my
6 steps slip. I cal'd on thee,
for thou wilt heare, God, heare my speech,
incline thine eare to mee.

7 O thou that sav'st by thy right hand,
thy merveilous-mercyes,

shew

ſhew vnto them that truſt in thee,
   from ſuch as 'gainſt them riſe.

(2)

8 As apple of thine eye mee keepe.
   In thy wings ſhade mee hide.
9 From wicked who mee waſt : my foes
   in heart are on each ſide.
10 Cloſ'd in their fat they are: & they
   ſpeak with their mouth proudly.
11 They round us in our ſtepps: they ſet
   on earth their bow'd downe eye.
12 His likenes as a lion is,
   that greedy is to teare,
in ſecret places lurking as
   hee a young lion were.
13 Him, in his ſight, riſe, diſappoynt
   make him bow downe o Lord,
doe thou my ſoule deliver from
   the wicked one, thy ſword,
14 From mortall men thine hand, o Lord
   from men that mortall are,
and of this paſſing-world, who have
   within this life their ſhare,
with thy hid treaſure furthermore
   whoſe belly thou filleſt:
their ſonnes are fil'd, & to their babes
   of wealth they leave the reſt.
15 In righteouſnes, thy favour I
   ſhall very clearely ſee,
and waking with thine image, I
   ſhall ſatiſſied bee.

C 3   PSALM

Pſalme 18

To the chiefe Muſician, a *pſalme* of Dauid, the ſervant of
the Lord, who ſpake the words of this Song, in the day that
the Lord deliuered him from the hands of all his enemies,
& from the hand of Saule, and hee Sayde,

ILe dearely love thee, Lord, my ſtrength.
  The Lord is my rock, and my towre
  and my deliverer, my God,
  I'le truſt in him *who is* my powre,
  My ſhield, & my ſalvationes-horne,

3 my high-fort; Who is prayſe worthy:
  I on the Lord will call, ſo ſhall
  I bee kept from mine enemye.

4 Deaths ſorrowes mee encompaſſed,
  mee fear'd the floods of ungodlie,

5 Hells pangs beſet me round abour,
  the ſnares of death prevented mee.

6 I in my ſtreights, cal'd on the Lord,
  and to my God cry'd: he did heare
  from his temple my voyce, my crye,
  before him came, unto his eare.

7 Then th' earth ſhooke, & quak't, & moūtaines
  roots moov'd, & were ſtird at his ire,

8 Vp from his noſtrils went a ſmoak,
  and from his mouth devouring fire:
  By it the coales inkindled were.

9 Likewiſe the heavens he dowre-bow'd,
  and he deſcended, & there was
  under his feet a gloomy cloud.

10 And he on cherub rode, and flew;
  yea he flew on the wings of winde.

11 His ſecret place hee darknes made

his

his covert that him round confinde,
Dark waters, & thick clouds of skies.

12 From brightnes,that before him was,
his thickned clouds did passe away,
hayl-stones and coales of fire did passe.

13 Also Iehovah thundered,
within the heavens,the most high
likewise his angry-voyce did give,
hayl-stones, and coales of fire *did fly.*

14 Yea he did out his arrows send,
and bruising he them scattered,
and lightnings hee did multiply,
likewise he them discomfited.

15 The waters channels then were seene,
and the foundationes of the world
appear'd;at thy rebuke,at blast,
of the breath of thy nostrils *Lord.*

(2)

16 Hee from above sent hee me took:
me out of waters-great he drew.

17 Hee from mine enemies-strong, & from
them which me hated did rescue:
For they were mightyer then I.

18 They mee prevented in the day
of my cloudy calamity;
but for me was the Lord a stay.

19 And hee me to large place brought forth:
hee sav'd mee, for he did delight

20 in mee. The Lord rewarded me
according as I did aright,
According to the cleannesse of

my

my hands, he recompenced mee.

21 For the wayes of the Lord I kept:
nor from my God went wickedlie.

22 For all his judgements mee before:
nor from me put I his decree.

23 With him I upright was, and kept
my selfe from mine iniquitie.

24 The Lord hath recompenced mee,
after my righteousnes therefore:
according to the cleannesse of
my hands that was his eyes before.

25 With mercifull, thou mercifull,
with upright thou deales uprightly.

26 With pure thou pure, thou also wilt
with froward turne thy selfe awry.

27 For thou wilt save th'afflicted folke:
but wilt the lofty looks suppresse.

28 For thou wilt light my lampe: the Lord,
my God will lighten my darknesse.

29 For by the I rann through a troupe,
and by my God leapt o're a wall.

30 Gods way is perfect: Gods word tryde:
that trust in him hee's shield to all.

31 For who is God except the Lord?
or who a rock, our God except?

32 Its God that girdeth me with strength,
and hee doth make my way perfect.

33 Like to the hyndes he makes my feet:
and on my high place maks me stand.

34 Mine armes doe break a bow of brasse;
so well to warre he learnes my hand.

35 The ſhield of thy ſalvation
   thou furthermore haſt given mee:
   and thy right-hand hath mee upheld,
   thy meeknes made mee great to bee.

36 Vnder mee thou makſt large my ſteps,
   ſo that mine anckles did not ſlyde

37 My foes purſu'de I, & them caught:
   nor turn'd I till they were deſtroyd,

38 I wounded them & they could not
   riſe up: under my feet they fell.

39 Becauſe that thou haſt girded mee
   with fortitude to the battel:
   Thou haſt ſubdued under mee,
   thoſe that did up againſt me riſe.

40 And my foes necks thou gaveſt mee,
   that I might waſt mine enemyes.

41 They cryde but there was none to ſave,
   to God, yet with no anſwer meet.

42 I beat them then as duſt i'th winde
   and caſt them out as dirt i'th ſtreet.

(4)

43 And thou from the contentions
   haſt of the people mee ſet free;
   thou of the heathen mad'ſt me head:
   people I knew not ſhall ſerve mee.

44 They'le at firſt hearing me obey:
   ſtrangers ſhall yield themſelvs to mee.

45 The ſtrangers ſhall conſume away,
   and from their cloſets frighted bee.

46 The Lord lives, and bleſt be my Rock,
   let my healths God exalted bee.

D   47 Its

47 It's God for mee that vengeance works,
and brings downe people under mee .

48 Mee from mine enemies he doth save:
and above those that 'gainst me went,
thou lift'st me up; and thou hast freed
mee from the man that's violent.

49 I with confession will therefore
unto thee render thanksgiving,
o Lord, among the heathen-folk;
and to thy name I'le prayses sing:

50 He giveth great deliverance
to his King, and doth shew mercy
to his annoynted, to David,
and to his seed eternally.

Psalme 19

To the chiefe musician a psalme of David.

THe heavens doe declare
the majesty of God:
also the firmament shews forth
his handy-work abroad.

2 Day speaks to day, knowledge
night hath to night declar'd.

3 There neither speach nor language is,
where their voyce is not heard.

4 Through all the earth their line
is gone forth, & unto
the utmost end of all the world,
their speaches reach also:
A Tabernacle hee
in them pitcht for the Sun.

5 Who Bridegroom like from's chamber goes
glad

glad Giants-race to run.

6 From heavens utmoſt end,
   his courſe and compaſſing;
to ends of it, & from the heat
   thereof is hid nothing.

(2)

7 The Lords law perfect is,
   the ſoule converting back:
Gods teſtimony faithfull is,
   makes wiſe who-wiſdome-lack.

8 The ſtatutes of the Lord,
   are right, & glad the heart:
the Lords commandement is pure,
   light doth to eyes impart.

9 Iehovahs feare is cleane,
   and doth indure for ever:
the judgements of the Lord are true,
   and righteous altogether.

10 Then gold, then much fine gold,
   more to be prized are,
then hony, & the hony-comb,
   ſweeter they are by farre.

11 Alſo thy ſervant is
   admoniſhed from hence:
and in the keeping of the ſame
   is a full recompence.

12 Who can his errors know?
   from ſecret faults cleanſe mee.

13 And from preſumptuous-ſins, let thou
   kept back thy ſervant bee:
Let them not beare the rule

in

in me, & then shall I
be perfect, and shall cleansed bee
from much iniquity.

14 Let the words of my mouth,
and the thoughts of my heart,
be pleasing with thee, Lord, my Rock
who my redeemer art.

Psalme 20

To the chiefe Musician, a psalme of David.

IEHOVAH heare thee in the day
of sore calamity,
the name of the God of Iacob
defend thee mightily.

2 Send thee help from his holy place
from Sion strengthen thee.

3 Minde all thy gifts, thy sacrifice
accepted let it bee.   Selah.

4 Grant thee according to thy heart,
all thy counsell fulfill.

5 In thy perfect salvation
with singing joy we will:
And we in the name of our God
our banners will erect:
when as all thy petitions
Iehovah shall effect.

6 Now I know, that Iehovah doth
save his annoynted-Deare:
with saving strength of his right hand
from his pure heav'n will heare.

7 In charrets some their confidence,
and some in horses set:

but

but we the name of Iehovah
    our God will not forget.
8 They are brought downe & fal'n: but we,
    rise and stand stedfastly.
9 Save Lord,& let the King us heare
    when as to him we cry.
            Psalme 21
    To the chiefe Musician a psalme
        of David.

IEHOVAH, in thy strength
    the King shall joyfull bee;
and joy in thy salvation
    how vehemently shall hee?
2 Thou of his heart to him
    hast granted the desire:
and thou hast not witholden back,
    what his lips did require.   Selah.
3 For thou dost with blessings
    of goodnes prevent him:
thou on his head of finest gold
    hast set a Diadem.
4 Of thee hee asked life,
    to him thou gav'st it free,
even length of days for evermore
    unto eternitie.
5 In thy salvation
    his glory hath bene great:
honour, and comely dignity
    thou hast upon him set.
6 For thou him blessings setst
    to perpetuitie:

            D 3

PSALM XXI.

Thou makſt him with thy countenance
    exceeding glad to bee.

7 Becauſe that in the Lord
    the King doth truſt, & hee
through mercy of the higheſt one,
    ſhall not removed bee.

8 The Lord ſhall finde out all
    that are thine enemies:
thy right hand alſo ſhall finde out
    thoſe that doe thee deſpiſe.

9 Thou ſetſt as fiery oven
    them in times of thine ire:
the Lord will ſwallow them in's wrath
    and them conſume with fire.

10 Thou wilt deſtroy the fruit,
    that doth proceed of them,
out of the earth: & their ſeed from
    among the Sonnes of men.

11 Becauſe they evill have
    intended againſt thee:
a wicked plot they have deviſ'd,
    but ſhall not able bee.

12 For thou wilt as a butt
    them ſet; & thou wilt place
thine arrows ready on thy ſtring,
    full right againſt their face.

13 Lord, in thy fortitude
    exalted bee on high:
and wee will ſing; yea prayſe with pſalmes
    thy mighty powr will wee.

PSAL.

PSALME XXII.

Pſalme 22
To the chiefe muſician upon *Aijeleth Shahar*
a pſalme of David.

MY God, my God, wherefore haſt thou
forſaken mee? & why,
art thou ſo farre from helping mee,
from the words of my cry?

2 O my God, I doe cry by day,
but mee thou doſt not heare;
and eke by night, & unto mee
no quiet reſt is there.

3 Neverthelesſe thou holy art,
who conſtantly doſt dwell,
within the thankfull prayſes of
thy people Iſraell.

4 Our fore-fathers in thee have put
aſſured confidence:
they truſted have, & thou to them
didſt give deliverance.

5 Vnto thee they did cry aloud,
and were delivered:
in thee they put their confidence,
and were not confounded.

6 But I a worme, & not a man;
of men an opprobrie,
and alſo of the people am
deſpiſ'd contempruouſlie.

7 All they that doe upon mee look,
a ſcoffe at mee doe make:
they with the lip doe make a mow,
the head in ſcorne they ſhake,

upō

8 Vpon the Lord he rold himselfe,
    let him now rid him quite:
let him deliver him, becaufe
    in him he doth delight.

9 But thou art hee that me out of
    the belly forth didft take:
when I was on my mothers breafts,
    to hope thou didft mee make.

10 Vnto thee from the tender-womb
    committed been have I:
yea thou haft been my mighty-God
    from my mothers belly.

(2)

11 Be thou not farre away from mee,
    for tribulation
exceeding great is neere at hand,
    for helper there is none.

12 Mee many buls on every fide
    about have compaffed:
the mighty- buls of Bafhan have
    mee round invironed.

13 They have with their wide-opened-mouths
    fo gaped mee upon;
like as it were a ravening
    and a roaring Lion.

14 As water I am poured-out,
    and all my bones fundred:
my heart in midft of my bowels,
    is like to wax melted.

15 My ftrength like a potfherd is dryde;
    and my tongue faft cleaveth

unto my jawes,& thou haft brought
   me to the duft of death.

16 For dogs have compaft me abour;
   th' affembly me befet
of the wicked; they pierced through
   my hands, alfo my feet.

17 My bones I may them number all:
   they lookt,they did me view.

18 My cloths among them they did part:
   and lot for my coat threw.

19 But thou Lord be not far, my ftrength,
   to help me haften thou.

20 My foule from fword,my darling from
   the powre of dogs refcue.

21 And from the mouth of the Lion
   give me falvation free:
for thou from hornes of Vnicornes
   anfwer haft given mee.

22 Thy name,I will declare to them
   that Brethren are to mee:
in midft of congregation
   I will give prayfe to thee.

(3)

23 Yee that doe feare the Lord prayfe him,
   all Iacobs feed prayfe yee,
him glorify,& dread him all
   yee Ifraels feed that bee.

24 For he the poors affliction
   loaths not,nor doth defpife;
nor hides his face from him, but heats
   when unto him hee cryes.

E   25 concern-

25 Concerning thee shall be my prayse
in the great assembly:
before them that him reverence
performe my vowes will I.

26 The meek shall eat & be suffic'd:
Iehovah prayse shall they
that doe him seek: your heart shall live
unto perpetuall aye.

27 All ends of th'earth remember shall
and turne unto the Lord:
and thee all heathen-families
to worship shall *accord*.

28 Because unto Iehovah doth
the kingdome appertaine:
and he among the nations
is ruler Soveraigne.

29 Earths-fat-ones, eat & worship shall:
all who to dust descend,
(though none can make alive his soule)
before his face shall bend.

30 With service a posterity
him shall attend upon;
to God it shall accounted bee
a generation.

31 Come shall they, & his righteousnes
by them declar'd shall bee,
unto a people yet unborne,
that done this thing hath hee.

23 *A Psalme of David.*

THe Lord to mee a shepheard is,
want therefore shall not I.

2 Hee

2 Hee in the folds of tender-graſſe,
  doth cauſe mee downe to lie:
 To waters calme me gently leads
3 Reſtore my ſoule doth hee:
  he doth in paths of righteouſnes:
  for his names ſake leade mee.
4 Yea though in valley of deaths ſhade
  I walk, none ill I'le feare:
  becauſe thou art with mee, thy rod,
  and ſtaffe my comfort are.
5 For mee a table thou haſt ſpread,
  in preſence of my foes:
  thou doſt annoynt my head with oyle,
  my cup it over-flowes.
6 Goodnes & mercy ſurely ſhall
  all my dayes follow mee:
  and in the Lords houſe I ſhall dwell
  ſo long as dayes ſhall bee.

   Pſalme **24**
  A pſalme of david.

THe earth Iehovahs is,
  and the fulneſſe of it:
 the habitable world, & they
  that there upon doe ſit.
2 Becauſe upon the ſeas,
  hee hath it firmly layd:
 and it upon the water-floods
  moſt ſollidly hath ſtayd.
3 The mountaine of the Lord,
  who ſhall thereto aſcend?
 and in his place of holynes,
    E 2
          who

who is it that shall stand?

4 The cleane in hands, & pure
   in heart;to vanity
who hath not lifted up his soule,
   nor sworne deceitfully.

5 From God he shall receive
   a benediction,
and righteousnes from the strong-God
   of his salvation.

6 This is the progenie
   of them that seek thy face:
of them that doe inquire for him:
   of Iacob 'tis the race.   Selah.

7 Yee gates lift-up your heads,
   and doors everlasting,
be yee lift up: & there into
   shall come the glorious-King.

8 Who is this glorious King?
   Iehovah, puissant,
and valiant, Iehovah is
   in battel valiant.

9 Yee gates lift-up your heads,
   and doors everlasting,
doe yee lift-up: & there into
   shall come the glorious-King.

10 Who is this glorious-King?
   loe, it is Iehovah
of warlike armies, hee the King
   of glory is; Selah.

Psalme 25
A psalme of David.

PSALM

PSALME XXV.

I Lift my foule to thee o Lord.
  My God I truft in thee,
let mee not be afham'd: nor let
  my foes joy over mee.
3 Yea, all that wait on thee fhall not,
  be fill'd with fhamefulnes:
but they fhall be afhamed all,
  who without caufe tranfgreffe.
4 Thy wayes, Iehovah, make mee know,
  thy paths make me difcerne.
5 Caufe mee my fteps to order well,
  in thy truth, & mee learne,
For thou God of my faving health,
  on thee I wait all day.
6 Thy bowels, Lord, & thy mercyes
  minde; for they are for aye.
7 Sinnes of my youth remember not,
  neither my trefpaffes:
after thy mercy minde thou mee
  o Lord for thy goodnes.
8 Good and upright God is, therefore
  will finners teach the way.
9 The meek he'le guide in judgement: &
  will teach the meek his way.
10 Iehovahs paths they mercy are,
  all of them truth alfo;
to them that keep his covenant,
  and teftimonies do.
                (2)
11 For thy names fake o Iehovah,
  freely doe thou remitt
          E 3   mine

mine owne perverse iniquitie:
 because that great is it.

12 Who fears the Lord, him hee will teach
 the way that he shall chuse.

13 his soule shall dwell at ease, his seed
 as heirs the earth shall vse.

14 The secret of God is with those
 that doe him reverence:
and of his covenant he them
 will give intelligence.

15 Mine eyes continually are
 upon Iehovah set:
for it is hee that will bring forth
 my feet out of the net.

16 Vnto me-wards turne thou thy face,
 and on mee mercy show:
because I solitary am
 afflicted poore also.

17 My hearts troubles inlarged are;
 from my distresse me bring.

18 See mine affliction,& my paine;
 and pardon all my sin.

19 Mark my foes; for they many are,
 and cruelly mee hate,

20 My soule keep,free mee;nor let mee
 be sham'd,who on thee wait.

21 Let soundnes,& uprightnesse keep
 mee: for I trust in thee.

22 Israel from his troubles all,
 o God, doe thou set free.
  25 A psalme of david.

PSA 2.

IVdge mee, o Lord, for I have walkt
   in mine integrity:
  and I have trusted in the Lord,
    therefore slyde shall not I.

2 Examine mee, Lord, & mee prove;
    my reins, & my heart try.

3 For thy grace is before mine eyes;
    and in thy truth walk I.

4 I sat not with vaine men, nor goe
    with men themselves that hide.

5 Evill mens company I hate:
    nor will with vile abide.

6 In cleannesse, Lord, I'le wash mine hands,
    so I'le thine altar round:

7 That I may preach with thankfull-voyce,
    and all thy prayses sound.

8 The habitation of thy house,
    Lord, dearly love doe I,
  the place and tabernacle of
    thy glorious majesty.

9 My soule with sinners gather not,
    with men of blood my life.

10 In whose hand 's guile, in whose right hand
    bribery is full rife.

11 Redeeme, & pitty mee; for I'le
    walk in mine uprightnesse.

12 My foot stands right: in th'assembly
    I will Iehovah blesse.

    27 *A* Psalme of David.

THe Lord my light, & my health is,
   what shall make me dismaid?

&c

PSALM XXVII.

The Lord is my lifes-strength, of whom
    should I *then* be afrayd?
2 When wicked men, mine enemies,
    and my foes in battel;
against mee come, to eate my flesh,
    themselves stumbled & fell.
3 If that an hoast against mee camp,
    my heart undaunted is:
if war against mee should arise,
    I am secure in this.
4 One thing of God I asked have,
    which I will still request:
that I may in the house of God,
    all dayes of my life rest:
To see the beauty of the Lord,
    and in his Temple seeke.
5 For in his tent in th'evill-day,
    hidden hee will mee keepe:
Hee will me hide in secrecy
    of his pavillion:
and will me highly lift upon
    the rocks-munition.
6 Moreover at this-time my head
    lifted on high shall bee,
above mine enemies, who doe
    about encompasse mee.
Therefore in's tent I'le sacrifice,
    of joye an offering,
unto Iehovah, sing will I,
    yea, I will prayses sing.

whe

(2)

7 When as I with my voyce doe cry,
     mee, o Iehovah, heare;
   have mercy alſo upon mee,
     and unto mee anſwer.

8 *When thou didſt ſay*, ſeek yee my face,
     my heart ſayd unto thee,
   thy countenance, o Iehovah,
     it ſhall be ſought by mee.

9 Hide not thy face from mee, nor off
     in wrath thy ſervant caſt:
   God of my health, leave, leave not mee,
     my helper been thou haſt.

10 My father & my mother both
     though they doe mee forſake,
   yet will Iehovah gathering
     unto himſelfe me take.

11 Iehovah, teach thou mee the way,
     and be a guide to mee
   in righteous path, becauſe of them
     that mine obſervers bee.

12 Give mee not up unto the will
     of my ſtreight-enemies:
   for witneſſe falſe againſt me ſtand,
     and breath out cruelties.

13 *I ſhould haue fainted*, had not I
     believed for to ſee,
   Iehovahs goodnes in the land
     of them that living bee.

14 Doe thou upon Iehovah waite:
     bee ſtabliſhed, & let

F   thine

thine heart be ſtrengthened,& thine hope
upon Iehovah ſet.

Pſalme 28.

A pſalme of David.

IEHOVAH,unto thee I cry,
my Rock,be thou not deafe me fro:
leſt thou be dumb from mee & I
be like them downe to pit that go.

2　Heare thou the voyce of my requeſt
for grace, when unto thee I cry:
when I lift up mine hands unto
thine Oracle of Sanctity.

3　With ill men draw me not away,
with workers of unrighteouſnes,
that with their neighbours peace doe ſpeak,
but in their hands is wickednes.

4　Give thou to them like to their works
and like the evill of their deeds:
give them like to their handy-works,
and render unto them their meeds.

5　Becauſe unto Iehovahs work
they did not wiſe-attention yeild,
neither unto his handy work,
them he will waſt,but not up-build.

6　The Lord be bleſt, for he hath heard
the voyce of my requeſts for grace.

7　God is my ſtrength,my ſhield,in him
my heart did truſt, & helpt I was:
Therefore my heart will gladnes ſhew,
and with my ſong I'le him confeſſe.

8　The Lord of his annoynted ones

their

their ſtrength, & towre of ſafety is.

9 Salvation to thy people give,
  and bleſſe thou thine inheritance,
  and ev'n unto eternity
  doe thou them feed & them advance.

This. After the common tunes.

Save *Lord,*thy people,& doe thou
  bleſſe thine inheritance:
and unto all eternity
  them feed & them advance.

Pſalme 29
A pſalme of David.

VNto the Lord doe yee aſcribe
  (o Sonnes of the mighty)
unto the *Lord* doe yee aſcribe
  glory & potency.
2 Vnto the Lord doe yee aſcribe
  his names glorious renowne,
in beauty of his holynes
  unto the Lord bow downe.
3 The mighty voyce of Iehovah
  upon the waters is:
the God of glory thundereth,
  God on great waters is.
4 Iehovahs voyce is powerfull,
  Gods voyce is glorious,
5 Gods voyce breaks Cedars:yea God breaks
  Cedars of Lebanus.
6 He makes them like a calſe to ſkip:

the

the mountaine Lebanon,
and like to a young Vnicorne
the hill of Syrion.
7 Gods voyce divides the flames of fire.
8 Iehovahs voyce doth make
the desart shake: the Lord doth cause
the Cadesh-desart shake.
9 The Lords voyce makes the hindes to calve,
and makes the forrest bare:
and in his temple every one
his glory doth declare.
10 The Lord sate on the flouds: the Lord
for ever sits as King.
11 God to his folk gives strength: the Lord
his folk with peace blessing.

Psalme 30

A Psalme & Song, *at* the dedication
of the house of David.

IEHOVAH, I will thee extoll,
for thou hast lift up mee;
and over mee thou hast not made
my foes joyfull to bee.
2 O Lord my God, to thee I cry'de
and thou hast made mee whole.
3 Out of the grave, o Iehovah,
thou hast brought up my soule:
Thou mad'st mee live, I went not downe
4 to pit. Sing to the Lord,
(yee his Saints) & give thanks when yee
his holynes record.
5 For but a moment in his wrath;

life

life in his love doth ſtay:
weeping may lodge with us a night
but joye at break of day.

6 I ſayd in my proſperity,
I ſhall be moved never.

7 Lord by thy favour thou haſt made
my mountaine ſtand faſt ever:
Thou hidſt thy face,I troubled was.

8 I unto thee did cry,
o Lord: alſo my humble ſuit
unto the Lord made I.

9 What gaine is in my blood; when I
into the pit goe downe?
ſhall duſt give glory unto thee?
ſhall it thy truth make knowne?

10 Doe thou mee o Iehovah,heare,
and on mee mercy have:
Iehovah,o bee thou to mee
an helper me to ſave.

11 Thou into dancing for my ſake
converted haſt my ſadnes:
my ſackcloth thou unlooſed haſt,
and girded me with gladnes:

12 That ſing to thee my glory may,
and may not ſilent bee:
o Lord my God,I will give thanks
for evermore to thee.

Pſalme 31
To the chief Muſician, a pſalme
of David.

F 3   PSALM

IN thee, o Lord, I put my truſt,
  let me be ſhamed never:
according to thy righteouſnes
  o doe thou mee deliver.
2 Bow downe to mee thine eare, with ſpeed
  let mee deliverance have:
be thou my ſtrong rock, for an houſe
  of defence mee to ſave.
3 Becauſe thou unto mee a rock
  and my fortreſſe wilt bee:
therefore for thy names ſake doe thou,
  leade mee & guide thou mee.
4 Doe thou mee pull out of the net,
  which they have for mee layd
ſo privily: becauſe that thou
  art to mee a ſure ayd.
5 Into thy hands my ſpirit I
  repoſing doe commit:
Iehovah God of verity,
  thou haſt redeemed it.
6 I hated them that have regard
  to lying vanity:
7 but I in God truſt. I'le be glad,
  and joy in thy mercy:
Becauſe thou haſt conſidered
  my afflicting diſtreſſe;
thou haſt my ſoule acknowledged
  in painfull anguiſhes;
8 And thou haſt not incloſed mee
  within the enemies hand:
thou mad'ſt my feet within the place

of

of liberty to ſtand.

(2)

9 Have mercy upon mee,o Lord,
  for in diſtreſſe am I,
 wIth grief mine eye conſumed is,
  my ſoule & my belly.
10 For my life with grief & my years
  with ſighs are conſumed:
 becauſe of my ſin,my ſtrength failes,
  and my bones are waſted.
11 To all my foes I was a ſcorne,
  chiefly my neighbours to;
 a feare to freinds: they that ſaw mee
  without, did flye me fro.
12 I am forgot as a dead man
  that's out of memory:
 and like a veſſel that is broke
  ev'n ſuch a one am I.
13 Becauſe that I of many men
  the ſlandeŗing did heare,
 round about me on every ſide
  there was exceeding feare:
 While as that they did againſt mee
  counſell together take,
 they craftily have purpoſed
  my life away to make.
14 But o Iehovah,I in thee
  my confidence have put
15 I ſayd thou art my God. My times
  within thy hand *are ſhut*:
 From the hands of mine enemies

doe

doe thou deliver mee,
and from the men who meeagainst
my perfecuters bee.

(5)

15 Thy countenance for to fhine forth
upon thy fervant make:
o give to me falvation
even for thy mercy fake.

17 Let me not be afham'd, o Lord,
for cal'd on thee I have:
let wicked men be fham'd, let them
be filent in the grave.

18 Let lying lips be filenced,
that againft men upright
doe fpeak fuch things as greivous are,
in pride, & in defpight.

19 How great 's thy goodnes, thou for the
that feare thee haft hidden:
which thou work'ft for them that thee truft,
before the Sonnes of men.

20 Thou in the fecretof thy face,
fhalt hide them from mans pride:
in a pavillion, from the ftrife
of tongues, thou wilt them hide.

21 O let Iehovah bleffed be;
for he hath fhewed mee
his loving kindnes wonderfull
in a fenced-cittie.

22 For I in haft fayd, I am caft
from the fight of thine eyes:
yet thou heardft the voyce of my fuit,

when

when to thee were my cryes.
23 O love the Lord all ye his Saints:
    becaufe the Lord doth guard
the faithfull, but the proud doer
    doth plenteoufly reward.
24 See that yee be encouraged,
    and let your heart wax ftrong:
all whofoever hopefully
    doe for Iehovah long.

   32 A *pfalme* of David, Mafchil.
O Bleffed is the man who hath
    his trefpaffe pardoned,
and he *whofe* aberration
    is wholly covered,
2 O bleffed is the man to whom
    the Lord imputes not fin:
and he who fuch a fpirit hath
    that guile is not therein.
3 When I kept filence then my bones,
    began to weare away,
with age; by meanes of my roaring
    continuing all the day.
4 For day & night thy hand on mee,
    heavily did indure:
into the drought of Summer time
    turned is my moifture.   Selah.
5 Mine aberration unto thee
    I have acknowledged,
and mine iniquity I have
    not clofely covered:
Againft my felfe my fin, fayd I,
            G   I will

I will to God confeſſe,
  and thou didſt the iniquitie
    forgive of my treſpaſſe.   **Selah,**

6 For this each godly one to thee
  in finding time ſhall pray.
  ſurely in floods of waters great,
    come nigh him ſhall not they.

7 Thou art my hyding-place, thou ſhalt
  from trouble ſave me out:
  thou with ſongs of deliverance
    ſhalt compaſſe me about.

8 I will inſtruct thee, alſo teach
  thee in the way will I
  which thou ſhalt goe: I will to thee
    give counſell with mine eye.

9 Like to the horſe & mule, which have
  noe knowledge be not yee:
  whoſe mouths are held with bridle-bit,
    that come not neere to thee.

10 To thoſe men that ungodly are,
  their ſorrows doe abound:
  but him that truſteth in the Lord,
    mercy ſhall compaſſe round.

11 Be in Iehovah joyfull yee,
  yee righteous ones rejoyce;
  and all that are upright in heart
    ſhout yee with joyfull voyce.

pſalme 33

Yee juſt in God rejoyce,
  praiſe well th'upright doth ſute:
2 Prayſe God with Harp, with pſaltry ſing

to him, on ten ftring'd lute.

3 Sing to him a new fong,
    aloud play fkilfully.

4 For the Lords word is right: and all
    his works in verity.

5 He loveth righteoufnes,
    and alfo equity:
  the earth replenifhed is with
    the Lords benignity.

6 By the word of the Lord
    the heavens had their frame,
  and by the fpirit of his mouth,
    all the hoft of the fame.

7 The waters of the feas,
    he gathers as an heape;
  together as in ftore-houfes
    he layeth up the deepe.

8 Be all the earth in feare,
    becaufe of Iehovah:
  let all the dwellers of the world
    before him ftand in awe.

9 Becaufe he did but fpeak
    the word, & it was made:
  he gave out the commandement,
    and it was firmly ftay'd.

10 The Lord to nought doth bring
    the nations counfell; hee
  devifes of the people makes
    of none effect to bee.

11 The counfell of the Lord
    abide for ever fhall,

the cogitations of his heart
to generations all.

(2)

12 O blessed nation,
   whose God Iehovah is:
and people whom for heritage
   chosen hee hath for his.

13 The Lord from heaven looks,
   all Sonnes of men views well.

14 From his firme dwelling hee looks forth,
   on all that on earth dwell.

15 The hearts of all of them
   alike he fashioneth:
and all their operations
   he well considereth.

16 By multitude of hoast
   there is no King saved:
nor is by multitude of strength
   the strong delivered.

17 A horse a vaine thing is
   to be a saviour:
nor shall he work deliverance
   by greatnes of his power.

18 On them that doe him feare
   loe, is Iehovahs eye:
upon them that doe place their hope
   on his benignity.

19 To save alive in dearth,
   and their soule from death free.

20 Our soule doth for Iehovah wayt,
   our help, & shield is hee.

21 For our heart joyes in him:
for in's pure name truſt wee.
22 Let thy mercy (Lord)be on us:
like as we truſt in thee.

Pſalme 34

A *pſalme* of David,whē he changed his behaviour
before Abimelech,who drove him away
& he departed.

ILe bleſſe God alwayes,his prayſe ſhall
ſtill in my mouth be had.
2 My ſoule ſhall boaſt in God:the meeke
ſhall heare *this* & bee glad.
3 Exalt the Lord with mee,his name
let us together advance.
4 I ſoughr,God heard, who gave from all
my fears deliverance.
5 Him they beheld, & light'ned were,
nor ſham'd were their faces.
6 This poore man cry'd,the Lord him heard,
and freed from all diſtreſſe.
7 His camp about them round doth pitch
the Angell of the Lord;
who doe him feare;and to them doth
deliverance afford.
8 O taſt,alſo conſider yee,
that God is good:o bleſt,
that man is ever whoſe hope doth
for ſafety in him reſt.
9 O ſtand in feare of Iehovah,
his holy ones who bee.
becauſe that ſuch as doe him feare

G 3

not

not any want shall see.

10 The Lions young doe suffer lack,
    and suffer hungering:
  but they that seek Iehovah, shall
    not want any good thing.

(2)

11 I will you teach to feare the Lord:
    come children hark to mee.

12 Who is the man that willeth life:
    and loves good dayes to see?

13 Thy tongue from evill,& thy lips
    from speaking guile keep thou.

14 Depart from evill & doe good:
    seek peace,and it follow.

15 Vpon the men that righteous are
    the Lord doth set his eye:
  and likewise he doth bow his eare
    when unto him they cry.

16 Iehovahs face is set against
    them that doe wickedly:
  that he of them from off the earth
    may cut the memory.

17 They cry'd, God heard,& set them free,
    from their distresses all.

18 To broken hearts the Lord is neere,
    and contrite save he shall.

19 The just mans sorrows many are,
    from all God sets him free.

20 Hee kepeth all his bones, that none
    of them shall broken bee.

21 Evill shall certainly bring death
    the wicked man upon:
                       and

and thofe that hate the juft fhall come
   to defolation.
22 The foules of them that doe him ferve,
   Iehovah doth redeeme:
nor any fhall be defolate,
   that put their truft in him.

   35 *A pfalme* of David.

PLead, Lord, with them that with me plead:
  fight againft them that fight with mee.
2 Of fhield & buckler take thou hold,
  ftand up my helper for to bee.
3   Draw out the fpeare & ftop the way
  'gainft them that my purfuers bee:
  and doe thou fay unto my foule
  I am falvation unto thee.
4   Let them confounded be,& fham'd,
  that feek my foule how they may fpill:
  let them be turned back & fham'd
  that in their thoughts devife mine ill.
5   As chaffe before the winde,let them
  be,& Gods Angell them driving.
6 Let their way dark & flippery bee,
  and the Lords Angell them chafing.
7   For in a pit without a caufe,
  they hidden have for me a net:
  which they without a caufe have digg'd
  that they there in my foule may get.
8   Let unknowne ruin come on him,
  and let his net that he doth hide,
  himfelfe infnare: let him into
  the very fame deftruction flyde.

9   My soule shall in the Lord be glad:
in his salvation joyfull bee

10 And all my bones shall also say,
o Lord, who is like unto thee?
  Who from the stronger then himselfe
the poore afflicted settest free:
the poore afflicted & needy,
from such as spoylers of him bee.

(2)

11 False witnesses did up arise:
what I knew not they charg'd on mee.

12 Evill for good they mee repay'd,
whereby my soule might spoyled bee,

13 But I, when they were sick, was cloath'd
with sackcloath, & I afflicted
my soule with fasting, & my pray'r
into my bosom returned.

14 I walked as if he had been
my neere freind or mine owne brother:
I heavily bow'd downe as one
that mourneth for his owne mother.

15 But they in mine adversity
rejoyced, & they gathered
themselves together: yea abjects
themselves against mee gathered;
  And I was ignorant *hereof*,
and they unceasantly mee teare,

16 With hypocrites, mockers in feasts;
at me their teeth they gnashing were.

17 How long o Lord wilt thou look on?
my soule from their destructions,

o doe

o doe thou fet at liberty,
mine only one from the Lions.

18   I freely will give thanks to thee
within the congregation great:
and I thy prayfes will fet forth
where there be many people met.

19   Thofe that are wrongfully my foes,
let them not rejoyce over mee:
neither let them wink with the eye,
that are my haters cauflefly.

20   Becaufe that they doe not fpeak peace:
but in their thoughts they doe invent
deceitfull matters againft them
that in the land for peace are bent.

21   Gainft me they op'ned their mouths wide,
& fayd,ah,ah our eye it faw.

22   Thou faw'ft it(Lord)hold not thy peace:
Lord,from me be not far away.

23   Stirre up & wake to my judgement,
my God & my Lord, to my plea.

24   After thy juftice,judge me,Lord
my God,left or'e me joy fhould they.

25   Let them not fay within their hearts,
aha,our foules defire have wee:
we now have fwallowed him up,
o let them never fay of mee.

25   Sham'd let them be & confounded
joyntly,who at my hurt are glad:
let them that 'gainft me magnify,
with fhame & difhonour be clad.

27   Let them for joy fhout,& be glad

H

that

that favour doe my righteous cause:
yea, let them say continually,
extolled be the Lord with prayse,
   Who doth in the prosperity
of his servants his pleasure stay
23 And my tongue of thy justice shall,
and of thy prayse speake all the day.

     Psalme 36.
To the chief Musician a psalme of David,
    the servant of the Lord.

THe trespasse of the wicked one
   saith in assured-wise:
within my heart, the feare of God
   is not before his eyes.
2 For in his eyes he sooths himselfe:
   his sin is found meane while
3 hatefull. The words of his mouth are
   iniquity & guile:
He to be wise, to doe good leaves.
4   He mischief plotts on's bed,
he sets himselfe in way not good:
   he hath not ill hated.

     (2)
5 Thy mercy (Lord)in heaven is,
   to clouds thy faithfullnes.
6 Thy judgements a great deep, like great
   mountains thy righteousnes:
Thou savest man & beast,o Lord.
7   How pretious is thy grace,
therefore in shadow of thy wings
   mens sonnes their trust doe place.

              They

8 They of the fatnes of thy houſe
  unto the full ſhall take:
and of the river of thy joyes
  to drink thou ſhalt them make.
9 For with thee is the ſpring of life:
  in thy light wee'll ſee light.
10 To them that know thee ſtretch thy grace;
  to right in heart thy right.
11 Let no proud foot againſt me come,
  nor wicked hand move mee.
12 Wrong doers there are fal'n:caſt downe,
  and rayſ'd they cannot bee,

37 **A** Pſalme of David.

FRet not thy ſelfe becauſe of thoſe
  that evill workers bee,
nor envious bee againſt the men
  that work iniquitie.
2 For like unto the graſſe they ſhall
  be cut downe,ſuddenly:
and like unto the tender herb
  they withering ſhall dye.
3 Vpon the Lord put thou thy truſt,
  and bee thou doing good,
ſo ſhalt thou dwell within the land,
  and ſure thou ſhalt have food.
4 See that thou ſet thy hearts delight
  alſo upon the Lord,
and the deſyers of thy heart
  to thee he will afford.
5 Truſt in the Lord: & hee'l it work,
  to him commit thy way.

H 2   6 As

6 As light thy justice hee'l bring forth,
      thy judgement as noone day.

7 Rest in Iehovah, & for him
      with patience doe thou stay:
   fret not thy selfe because of him
      who prospers in his way,
   Nor at the man, who brings to passe
      the crafts he doth devise.

8 Cease ire, & wrath leave: to doe ill
      thy selfe fret in no wise.

9 For evil doers shall be made
      by cutting downe to fall:
   but those that wayt upon the Lord,
      the land inherit shall.

                (2)

10 For yet a litle while, & then
      the wicked shall not *bee*:
    yea, thou shait diligently mark
      his place, & it not see.

11 But meek ones the inheritance
      shall of the earth possesse:
    also they shall themselves delight
      in multitude of peace.

12 The wicked plotts against the just,
      gnashing at him his teeth.

13 The Lord shall laugh at him: because
      his day coming he seeth.

14 The wicked have drawne out their sword,
      & bent their bowe have they,
    to cast the poor & needy downe,
      to kill th'upright in way.

                                        15 their

15 Their sword shall enter their owne heart,
  their bowes shall broken bee.
16 The just mans little, better *is*
  then wickeds treasurie.
17 For th'armes of wicked shall be broke:
  the Lord the just doth stay.
18 The Lord doth know upright mens dayes:
  and their lot is for aye.
19 Neither shall they ashamed bee
  in any time of ill:
  and when the dayes of famine come,
  they then shall have their fill.
20 But wicked,& foes of the Lord
  as lambs fat shall decay:
  they shall consume:yea into smoake
  they shall consume away.
(3)
21 The man ungodly borroweth,
  but he doth not repay:
  but he that righteous is doth shew
  mercy,& gives away,
22 For such as of him blessed bee,
  the earth inherit shall,
  and they that of him cursed are,
  by cutting downe shall fall.
23 The foot-steps of a godly man
  they are by Iehovah
  established: & also hee
  delighteth in his way.
24 Although he fall,yet shall he not
  be utterly downe cast:
                H 3   because

becaufe Iehovah with his hand
  doth underprop him faft.
25 I have been young & now am old;
  yet have I never feen
the juft man left, nor that his feed
  for bread have beggars been.
26 But every day hee's mercifull,
  and lends: his feed is bleft.
27 Depart from evill,& doe good:
  and ever dwell at reft.
28 Becaufe the Lord doth judgement love,
  his Saints forfakes not hee;
kept ever are they: but cut off
  the finners feed fhall bee.
29 The juft inherit fhall the land,
  and therein ever dwell.
30 The juft mans mouth wifdome doth fpeak,
  his tongue doth judgement tell.
31 The law of his God is in's heart:
  none of his fteps flideth.
32 The wicked watcheth for the juft,
  and him to flay feeketh .
33 Iehovah will not fuch a one
  relinquifh in his hand,
neither will he condemne him when
  adjudged he doth ftand.
(4)
34 Wayt on the Lord,& keep his way,
  and hee fhall thee exalt
th'earth to inherit: when cut off
  the wicked fee thou fhalt.

35 The

35 The wicked men I have beheld
    in mighty pow'r to bee:
also himsefe spreading abroad
    like to a green-bay-tree.

36 Neverthelesse he past away,
    and loe, then was not hee;
moreover I did seek for him,
    but found hee could not bee.

37 Take notice of the perfect man,
    and the upright attend:
because that unto such a man
    peace is his latter end.

38 But such men that transgressors are
    together perish shall:
the latter end shall be cut off
    of the ungodly all,

39 But the salvation of the just
    doth of Iehovah come:
he is their strength to them in times
    that are most troublesome.

40 Yea, help & free them will the Lord:
    he shall deliver them
from wiced men, because that they
    doe put their trust in him.

Psalme 38
A psalme of David,
to bring to remembrance.

LORD, in thy wrath rebuke me not:
    nor in thy hot rage chasten mee.

2 Because thine hand doth presse me sore:
    and in me thy shafts fastened bee.

3 There

3   *There is* no soundnes in my flesh,
because thine anger I am in:
nor *is there* any rest within
my bones, by reason of my sin.

4   Because that mine iniquityes
ascended are above my head:
like as an heavy burden, they
to heavy upon me are layd.

5   My wounds stink, *and* corrupt they be:
my foolishnes doth make it so.

6   I troubled am, & much bow'd downe,
all the day long I mourning goe.

7   For with foule sores my loynes are fill'd:
& in my flesh *is* no soundnes.

8   I'me weak & broken sore; I roar'd
because of my hearts restlesnes.

9   All my desire's before thee, Lord;
nor is my groaning hid from thee.

10 My heart doth pant, my strength me fails:
& mine eye sight is gone from mee.

(2)

11   My freinds & lovers from my sore
stand off: off stand my kinsmen eke.

12 And they lay snares that seek my life,
that seek my hurt, they mischief speak,
    And all day long imagin guile,

13 But as one deafe, I did not heare,
and as a dumb man I became
as if his mouth not open were.

14   Thus was I as man that heares not,
& in whose mouth reproofes none were.

15 because

15 Becauſe o Lord, in thee I hope:
   o Lord my God, thou wilt mee heare.

16   For ſayd I, leſt or'e me they joy:
   when my foot ſlips, they vaunt the more

17   themſelves 'gainſt me. For I to halt
   am neere, my grief's ſtill mee before.

18   For my tranſgreſſion I'le declare;
   I for my ſins will ſorry bee.

19 But yet my lively foes are ſtrong,
   who falſly hate me, multiplie.

20   Moreover they that doe repay
   evill in ſtead of good to mee,
   becauſe I follow what is good,
   to mee they adverſaryes bee.

21   Iehovah, doe not mee forſake:
   my God o doe not farre depart

22 from mee. Make haſt unto mine ayd,
   o Lord who my ſalvation art.

Pſalme 39

To the chief muſician, *even* to Ieduthun,
a Pſalme of David.

I Sayd, I will look to my wayes,
   leſt I ſin with my tongue:
I'le keep my mouth with bit, while I
   the wicked am among.

2 With ſilence tyed was my tongue,
   my mouth I did refraine,
From ſpeaking that thing which is good,
   and ſtirred was my paine.

3 Mine heart within me waxed hot,
   while I was muſing long,

I   inkindled

PSALM xxx ix.

inkindled in me was the fire;
   then fpake I with my tongue.

4 Mine end, o Lord, & of my dayes
    let mee the meafure learne;
that what a momentany thing
    I am I may difcerne.

5 Behold thou mad'ft my dayes a fpan,
    mine age as nought to thee:
furely each man at's beft eftate,
    is wholly vanity.   Selah.

6 Sure in a vaine fhow walketh man;
    fure ftir'd in vaine they are:
he heaps up riches,& knows not
    who fhall the fame gather.

(2)

7 And now, o Lord what wayt I for?
    my hope is upon thee.

8 Free me from all my trefpaffes:
    the fooles fcorne make not mee.

9 I was dumb nor opned my mouth,
    this done becaufe thou haft.

10 Remove thy ftroke away fom mee:
    by thy hands blow I waft.

11 When with rebukes thou doft correct
    man for iniquity;
thou blaft's his beauty like a moth:
    fure each man 's vanity.   Selah.

12 Heare my pray'r, Lord, hark to my cry,
    be not ftill at my tears:
for ftranger, & pilgrim with thee,
    I 'me, as all my fathers.

13 O turne aſide a while from mee,
  that I may ſtrength recall:
before I doe depart from hence,
  and be noe more at all.

Pſalme 40.
To the chief muſician, a pſalme
of David.

WIth expectation for the Lord
  I wayted patiently,
and hee inclined unto mee.
  alſo he heard my cry.

2 He brought mee out of dreadfull-pit,
  out of the miery clay:
and ſet my feet upon a rock,
  hee ſtabliſhed my way.

3 And in my mouth put a new ſong,
  of prayſe our God unto:
many ſhall ſee, & feare, upon
  the Lord ſhall truſt alſo.

4 Bleſt is the man that on the Lord
  maketh his truſt abide:
nor doth the proud reſpect, nor ſuch
  to lies as turne aſide.

5 O thou Iehovah, thou my God,
  haſt many a wonder wrought:
and likewiſe towards us thou haſt
  conceived many a thought.
Their ſumme cannot be reck'ned up
  in order unto thee:
would I declare & ſpeak *of them*,
  beyond account they bee.

6 Thou

PSALM xl.

6 Thou sacrifice & offering
    wouldst not; thou boar'st mine eare:
  burnt offring,& sin offering
    thou neither didst requere.

7 Then sayd I: loe,I come: ith books
    rolle it is writt of mee.

8 To doe thy will,God, I delight:
    thy laws in my heart bee.

9 In the great congregation
    thy righteousnes I show:
  loe,I have not refraynd my lips,
    Iehovah, thou dost know.

10 I have not hid thy righteousnes
    within my heart alone:
  I have declar'd thy faithfullnes
    and thy salvation:
  Thy mercy nor thy truth have I
    from the great Church conceald.

11 Let not thy tender mercyes bee
    from mee o Lord with-held.
  Let both thy kindnes & thy truth
    keep me my life throughout.

12 Because innumerable ills
    have compast mee about:
  My sins have caught me so that I
    not able am to see:
  more are they then hairs of my head,
    therefore my heart fails mee

(3)

13 Be pleas'd Lord, to deliver mee

to

to help me Lord make haft.

14 At once abafht & fham'd let bee
   who feek my foule to wafte:
   Let them be driven back,& fham'd,
   that wifh me mifery.

15 Let them be wafte, to quit their fhame,
   that fay to me,fy fy.

16 Let all be glad, & joy in thee,
   that feek thee: let them fay
   who thy falvation love, the Lord
   be magnifyde alway.

17 I both diftreft & needy am,
   the Lord yet thinks on mee:
   my help & my deliverer thou
   my God, doe not tarry.

Pfalme 41
To the chief mufician, a pfalme
of David.

BLeffed is hee that wifely doth
   unto the poore attend:
   the Lord will him deliverance
   in time of trouble fend.

2 Him God will keep, & make to live,
   on earth hee bleft fhall be,
   nor doe thou him unto the will
   give of his enemie.

3 Vpon the bed of languifhing,
   the Lord will ftrengthen him:
   thou alfo wilt make all his bed
   within his ficknes time.

4 I fayd, Iehouah, o be thou
   I 3   merciful

mercifull unto mee;
heale thou my foule, becaufe that I
have finned againft thee.
5 Thofe men that be mine enemies,
with evill mee defame:
when will the time come hee fhall dye,
and perifh fhall his name?
6 And if he come to fee *mee*, hee
fpeaks vanity: his heart
fin to it felfe heaps, when hee goes
forth hee doth it impart.
(2)
7 All that me hate, againft mee they
together whifper ftill:
againft me they imagin doe
to mee malicious ill.
8 *Thus doe they fay* fome ill difeafe,
unto him cleaveth fore:
and *fcing now* he lyeth downe,
he fhall rife up noe more.
9 Moreover my familiar freind,
on whom my truft I fet,
his heele againft mee lifted up,
who of my bread did eat.
10 But Lord me pitty, & mee rayfe,
that I may them requite.
11 By this I know affuredly,
in mee thou doft delight:
For o're mee triumphs not my foe.
12   And mee, thou doft mee ftay,
in mine integrity; & fet'ft

mee

mee thee before for aye.
13 Bleſt hath Iehovah Iſraels God
   from everlaſting *been,*
  alſo unto everlaſting:
   Amen, yea and Amen.

THE

Second Booke.

PSALME 42

To the chief muſician, *Maſchil,* for the
Sonnes of Korah.

L Ike as the Hart panting doth bray
   after the water brooks,
  even in ſuch wiſe o God, my ſoule,
   after thee panting looks.
2 For God, even for the liuing God,
   my ſoule it thirſteth ſore:
  oh when ſhall I come & appeare,
   the face of God before.
3 My teares have been unto mee meat,
   by night alſo by day,
  while all the day they unto mee
   where is thy God doe ſay.
4 When as I doe in minde record
   theſe things, then me upon
  I doe my ſoule out poure, for I
   with multitude had gone:
  With them unto Gods houſe I went,
   with voyce of joy & prayſe:

                    I with

I with a multitude did goe
    that did keepe-holy-days.
5 My foule why art caſt downe?& art
    ſtirr‘d in mee: thy hope place
in God, for yet him prayſe I ſhall
    for the help of his face.

(2)

6 My God, my foule in mee‘s caſt downe,
    therefore thee minde I will
from Iordanes & Hermonites land,
    and from the litle hill.
7 At the noyſe of thy water ſpouts
    deep unto deep doth call:
thy waves they are gone over mee,
    alſo thy billowes all.
8 His loving kindnes yet the Lord
    command will in the day:
a nd in the night his ſong with mee,
    to my lifes God I‘le pray.
9 I unto God will ſay, my Rock
    why haſt thou forgot mee?
why goe I ſad, by reaſon of
    preſſure of th‘ enemie.
10 As with a ſword within my bones
    my foes reproach mee do:
while all the day, where is thy God?
    they doe ſay mee unto.
11 My foule o wherefore doſt thou bowe
    thy ſelfe downe heavily;
and wherefore in mee makeſt thou
    a ſtirr tumultuouſly?

Hope

Hope thou in God, becauſe I ſhall
   with prayſe him yet advance:
who is my God, alſo he is
   health of my countenance.

Pſalme 43.

IVdge me, o God, & plead my cauſe
   from nation mercyleſſe;
from the guilefull & man unjuſt,
   o ſend thou me redreſſe.

2 For of my ſtrength thou art the God,
   why caſt‘s thou mee thee fro:
why goe I mourning for the ſore
   oppreſſion of the foe?

3 Thy light o ſend out & thy truth,
   let them lead, & bring mee,
unto thy holy hill, & where
   thy tabernacles bee.

4 Then will I to Gods Altar goe,
   to God my joyes gladnes:
upon the Harp o God my God
   I will thy prayſe expreſſe.

5 My ſoule o wherfore doſt thou bowe
   thy ſelfe downe heavily;
and wherefore in mee makeſt thou
   a ſtirre tumultuouſly?
Hope thou in God, becauſe I ſhall
   with prayſe him yet advance:
who is my God, alſo he is
   health of my countenance.

Pſalme 44

To the chief muſician, for the ſonnes-
of Korah.   K   PSAL-

PSALM xliv.

WEE with our eares have heard, o God,
    our fathers have us told,
what works thou diddest in their dayes,
    in former dayes of old.

2 *How* thy hand drave the heathen out,
    and them thou planted haft;
how thou the people didſt afflict,
    and thou didſt them out-caſt.

3 For they got not by their owne ſword
    the lands poſſeſſion,
neither yet was it their owne arme
    wrought their ſalvation:
But thy right hand, thine arme alſo,
    thy countenances light;
becauſe that of thine owne good will
    thou didſt in them delight.

4 Thou art my king, o mighty God,
    thou doſt the ſame indure:
doe thou for Iacob by command
    deliverances procure.

5 Through thee as with a horne wee will
    puſh downe our enemies:
through thy name will wee tread them downe
    that up againſt us riſe.

6 Becauſe that *I* will in no wiſe
    any affiance have,
upon my bow, neither is it
    my ſword that ſhall mee ſave.

7 But from our enemies us thou ſav'd,
    and put our foes to ſhame.

8 In God wee boaſt all the day long,

                 and

and for aye prayſe thy name.   Selah.

(2)

9 But thou haſt caſt us off away,
   thou makeſt us alſo
to be aſham'd; neither doſt thou
   forth with our armies goe.
10 Vs from before the enemy
   thou makeſt back recoyle:
likewiſe they which our haters bee,
   for themſelves us doe ſpoyle.
11 Thou haſt us given like to ſheep
   to ſlaughter *that belong*:
alſo thou haſt us ſcattered
   the heathen folk among.
12 Thou doſt thy people ſet to ſale
   whereby no wealth doth riſe:
neither doſt thou obtaine increaſe
   of riches by their price.
13 Vnto our neighbours a reproach
   thou doeſt us expoſe,
a ſcorne we are & mocking ſtock,
   to them that us incloſe.
14 Among the heathen people thou
   a by word doſt us make:
alſo among the nations,
   at us their heads they ſhake.
15 Before me my confuſion
   it is continually,
and of my countenance the ſhame
   hath over covered mee.
16 Becauſe of his voyce that doth ſcorne,

K 2   and

and scoffingly despight:
by reason of the enemy,
    and selfe revenging wight.

(3)

17 All this is come on us, wee yet
    have not forgotten thee:
neither against thy covenant
    have wee dealt faithleslie.

18 Our heart is not turn'd back, nor have
    our steps from thy way stray'd;

19 Though us thou brake in dragons place,
    and hid us in deaths shade.

20 had wee forgot Gods name, or stretcht
    to a strange God our hands:

21 Shall not God search this out? for hee
    hearts secrets understands.

22 Yea, for thee all day wee are kil'd:
    counted as sheep to slay.

23 Awake, why sleepst thou, Lord? arise,
    cast us not off for aye.

24 Thy countenance away from us
    o wherefore dost thou hide?
of our grief & oppression
    forgetfull dost abide.

25 For our soule is bowd downe to dust:
    to earth cleaves our belly.

25 Rise for our help, & us redeeme,
    because of thy mercy.

Psalme 45

To the chief musician upon Shoshannim, for-
the sonnes of Korah, Maschil a song of loves.

PSAL.

PSALME xl, xlv.

MY heart good mater boyleth forth,
   my works touching the King
I speak: my tongue is as the pen
   of Scribe swiftly writing.
2 Fairer thou art then sonnes of men,
   grace in thy lips is shed:
because of this the Lord hath thee
   for evermore blessed.
3 Thy wasting sword o mighty one
   gird thou upon thy thigh:
thy glorious-magnificence,
   and comely majesty.
4 Ride forth upon the word of truth,
   meeknes & righteousnes:
and thy right hand shall lead thee forth
   in works of dreadfulnes.
5 Within the heart of the kings foes
   thine arrows piercing bee:
whereby the people overcome,
   shall fall downe under thee.
6 Thy throne o God, for ever is,
   the scepter of thy state
7 right scepter is. Iustice thou lov'st,
   but wickednes dost hate:
Because of this, God ev'n thy God
   hee hath annoynted thee,
with oyle of gladnes above them,
   that thy companions bee.
8 Myrrhs, Aloes, and Cassias *smell*,
   all of thy garments *had*:
out of the yvory pallaces

K 3   they

PSALM xlv.

wherby they made thee glad.
9 Amongst thine honourable maids
   kings daughters present were,
the Queen is set at thy right hand
   in fine gold of Ophir.

(2)

10 Harken o daughter, & behold,
   doe thou incline thine eare:
doe thou forget thine owne people,
   and house of thy father.
11 So shall the king delighting-rest
   himselfe in thy beautie:
and bowing downe worship thou him,
   because thy Lord is hee.
12 Then shall be present with a gift
   the daughter there of Tyre:
the wealthy ones of the people
   thy favour shall desire.
13 The daughter of the king she is
   all glorious within:
and with imbroderies of gold,
   her garments wrought have been.
14 She is led in unto the king
   in robes with needle wrought:
the virgins that doe follow her
   shall unto thee be brought.
15 They shall be brought forth with gladnes,
   also with rejoycing,
ſo shall they entrance have into
   the Pallace of the king.
16 Thy children shall in stead of those
   that were thy fathers bee: whom

whom thou mayſt place in all the earth
    in princely diginty.
17 Thy name remembred I will make
    through generations all:
therefore for ever & for aye
    the people prayſe thee ſhall.

Pſalme 46

To the chief muſician, for the ſonnes of-
    Korah, a ſong upon Alemoth.

GOD is our refuge, ſtrength, & help
    in troubles very neere.
2 Therefore we will not be afrayd,
    though th'earth removed were.
Though mountaines move to midſt of ſeas
3   Though waters roaring make
and troubled be, at whoſe ſwellings
    although the mountaines ſhake.   Selah.
4 There is a river ſtreames whereof
    ſhall rejoyce Gods city:
the holy place the tent wherin
    abideth the moſt high.
5 God is within the midſt of her,
    moved ſhee ſhall not bee:
God ſhall be unto her an help,
    in the morning early.
6 The nations made tumultuous noyſe,
    the kingdomes moved were:
he did give forth his thundering voyce
    the earth did melt *with feare.*
7 The God of Armies is with us
    th'eternall Iehovah:

                    the

the God of Iacob is for us
   a refuge high. Selah.
8 O come yee forth behold the works
      which Iehovah hath wrought,
   the fearfull desolations,
      which on the earth he brought.
9 Vnto the utmost ends of th'earth
      warres into peace hee turnes:
   the speare he cuts, the bowe he breaks,
      in fire the chariots burnes.
10 Be still, & know that I am God,
      exalted be will I
   among the heathen: through the earth
      I 'le be exalted hye.
11 The God of armyes is with us,
      th'eternall Iehovah:
   the God of Iacob is for us
      a refuge high. Selah.

Psalme 47.

To the chief musician: a psalme for the
Sonnes of Korah.

Clap hands all people, shout for joy,
   to God with voyce of singing mirth:
2 For high Iehovah fearfull is,
      a great King over all the earth.
3 People to us he doth subdue,
      and nations under our feet lay.
4 For us our heritage he chose,
      his deare Iacobs glory. Selah.
5 God is ascended with a shout:
      Iehovah with the trumpets noyse.

6 Sing

6 Sing psalmes to God, sing psalmes, sing-
  unto our King with singing voyce. (psalmes
7   For God is King of all the earth,
  sing yee psalmes of instruction:
8 Over the heathen God will reigne
  God sits his holy throne upon.
9   To the people of Abrahams-God
  Princes of peoples gathered bee,
  for shields of th'earth to God belong:
  he is exalted mightylie.

Psalme 48
To the chief musician, a song & psalme for
the sonnes of Korah.

GReat is Iehovah, & he is
  to be praysed greatly
within the city of our God,
  in his mountaine holy.
2 For situation beautifull,
  the joy of the whole earth
mount Sion; the great Kings city
  on the sides of the north.
3 God in her pallaces is knowne
  to be a refuge high.
4 For loe, the kings assembled were:
  they past together by.
5 They saw, & so they merveiled,
  were troubled, fled for feare.
6 Trembling seiz'd on them there & paine
  like her that childe doth beare.
7 The navies that of Tarshish are
  in pieces thou breakest:

L   even

ev'n with a very blaſt of winde
coming out of the eaſt.
8 As we heard, ſo we ſaw within
the Lord of hoaſts citty,
in our Gods citty, God will it
ſtabliſh eternally.   Selah.

(2)

9 O God we have had thoughts upon
thy free benignity,
within the very midle part
of thy temple holy,
10 According to thy name, o God
ſo is thy prayſe unto
the ends of earth: thy right hand 's full
of righteouſnes alſo.
11 Let the mountaine Sion rejoyce,
and triumph let them make
who are the daughters of Iudah,
ev'n for thy judgements ſake.
12 About the hill of Sion walk,
and goe about her yee,
and doe yee reckon up thereof
the tow'rs *that therein* bee.
13 Doe yee full well her bulwarks mark,
her Pallaces view well,
that to the generation
to come yee may it tell.
14 For this ſame God he is our God
for ever & for aye:
likewiſe unto the very death
he guides us in our way.

PSALM

Pfalme 49
To the chief mufician a pfalme for the
fonnes of Korah.

HEare this all people, all give eare
that dwell the world all o're.
2 Sonnes both of low, & higher men,
joyntly both rich & poore.
3 My mouth it fhall variety
of wifdome be fpeaking:
and my hearts meditation fhall
be of underftanding.
4 Vnto a fpeech proverbiall
I will mine eare incline;
I will alfo upon the Harp
open my dark doctrine.
5 Why fhould I be at all afrayd
in dayes that evill bee:
when that my heeles iniquity
about fhall compaffe mee.
(2)
6 Thofe men that make their great eftates
their ftay to truft unto,
who in the plenty of their wealth
themfelves doe boaft alfo:
7 Ther 's not a man *of them* that can
by any meanes redeeme
his brother, nor give unto God
enough to ranfome him.
8 So deare their foules redemption is
& ever ceafeth it.

L 2   9 That

9 That he should still for ever live
   and never see the pit.

10 For he doth see that wise man dye,
   the foole and brutish too
to perish, & their rich estate
   to others leave they doo.

11 They think their houses are for aye
   to generations all
their dwelling places, & their lands
   by their owne names they call.

12 Neverthelesse, in honour man,
   abideth not a night:
become he is just like unto
   the beasts that perish quite.

13 This their owne way their folly is;
   yet whatsoe're they say,
their successors that follow them
   doe well approve. Selah.

14 Like sheep so are they layd in grave,
   death shall them feed upon;
& th' upright over them in morn
   shall have dominion.
And from the place where they doe dwell,
   the beauty which they have,
shall utterly consume away
   in the devouring grave.

(3)

15 But surely Gods redemption
   unto my soule will give,
even from the power of the grave,
   for he will me receive.   Selah.

16 Be not afrayd when as a man
    in wealth is made to grow,
 and when the glory of his houfe
    abundantly doth flow.

17 Becaufe he fhall carry away
    nothing when he doth dye:
 neither fhall after him defcend
    ought of his dignity.

18 And albeit that he his foule
    in time of his life bleft,
 and men will prayfe thee, when as thou
    much of thy felfe makeft.

19 He fhall goe to his fathers race,
    they never fhall fee light.

20 Man in honour, & know'th not, is
    like beafts that perifh quite.

Pfalme 50.

A pfalme of Afaph.

THe mighty God, the Lord hath fpoke,
    and he the earth doth call,
 from the uprifing of the Sun,
    thereof unto the fall.

2 The mighty God hath clearely fhyn'd
    out of the mount Sion,
 which is of beauty excellent
    the full perfection.

3 Our God fhall come, and not be ftill
    fire fhall wafte in his fight;
 and round about him fhall be rayf'd
    a ftorme of vehement might.

4 His folk to judge he from above

L 3   calls

calls heavens,& earth likewise,

5 Bring mee my Saints,that cov'nant make
with mee by sacrifice.

6 And the heavens shall his righteousnes
shew forth apparentlie:
because the mighty God himselfe
a righteous judge will bee.   Selah.

(2)

7 Heare, o my people,& I will
speake,I will testify
also to thee o Israell,
I even thy God am I.

8 As for thy sacrifices I
will finde no fault with thee,
or thy burnt offrings,*which have been*
at all times before mee.

9 Ile take no bullocks,nor he-goates
from house,or foldes of thine.

10 For forrest beasts,& cattell all
on thousand hills are mine.

11 The flying foules of the mountaines
all of them doe I know:
and every wilde beast of the field
it is with mee also.

2 If I were hungry I would not
it unto thee declare:
for mine the habitable world,
and fullnes of it *are.*

5 Of bullocks eate the flesh,or drink
the blood of goates will I ?

14 Thanks offer unto God,& pay

thy

thy vowes to the moſt high.
15 And in the day of trouble ſore
doe thou unto mee cry,
and I will thee deliver, and
thou mee ſhalt glorify.
(3)
16 But to the wicked God ſayth, why
doſt thou the mention make
of my ſtatutes, why in thy mouth
ſhould'ſt thou my cov'nant take?
17 Sith thou doſt hate teaching and doſt
my words behinde thee caſt.
18 When thou didſt ſee a thief, then thou
with him conſented haſt;
And likewiſe with adulterers
thy part hath been the ſame.
19 Thy mouth to evill thou doſt give,
and guile thy tongue doth frame,
Thou ſitteſt, thou doſt ſpeake againſt
the man that is thy brother:
and thou doſt ſlaunder him that is
the ſonne of thine owne mother.
21 Theſe things haſt thou committed, and
in ſilence I kept cloſe:
that I was altogether like
thy ſelfe, thou didſt ſuppoſe:
I'le thee reprove, & in order
before thine eyes them ſet.
22 O therefore now conſider this
yee that doe God forget:
Leſt I you teare, & there be not

any

any deliverer.

23 He glorifieth mee that doth
    prayſe unto mee offer.

24 And hee that doth order *aright*
    his converſation,
to him will I give that hee may
    ſee Gods ſalvation.

Pſalme 51.

To the chief muſician, a pſalme of David, when
Nathan the prophet came unto him, after he
    had gone in unto Bathſheba.

HAve mercy upon mee o God,
    in thy loving kyndnes:
in multitude of thy mercyes
    blot out my treſpaſſes.

2 From mine iniquity doe thou
    waſh mee moſt perfectly,
and alſo from this ſin of mine
    doe thou mee puriſy.

3 Becauſe, of my tranſgreſſions
    my ſelfe doe take notice,
and ſin that I committed have
    before mee ever is.

4 Gainſt thee, thee only I have ſin'd
    this ill done thee before:
when thou ſpeakſt juſt thou art, & cleare
    when thou doſt judge therfore.

5 Behold, how in iniquity
    I did my ſhape receive:
alſo my mother *that mee bare*
    in ſin did mee conceive.

6 Behold

6 Behold, thou doſt deſire the truth
　within the inward part:
and thou ſhalt make mee wiſdome know
　in ſecret of my heart.

7 With hyſope doe me purify,
　I ſhall be cleanſed ſo:
doe thou mee waſh, & then I ſhall
　be whiter then the ſnow.

8 Of joy & of gladnes doe thou
　make me to heare the voyce:
that ſo the bones which thou haſt broke
　may cheerfully rejoyce.

9 From the beholding of my ſin
　hide thou away thy face:
alſo all mine iniquityes
　doe utterly deface.

(2)

10 A cleane heart (Lord) in me create,
　alſo a ſpirit right

11 in me renew. O caſt not mee
　away out of thy ſight;
Nor from me take thy holy ſpirit.

12 Reſtore the joy to mee
of thy ſalvation, & uphold
　me with thy ſpirit free.

13 Then will I teach thy wayes to thoſe
　that work iniquitie:
and by this meanes ſhall ſinners bee
　converted unto thee.

14 O God, God of my health, ſet mee
　free from bloud guiltines,

M　　　　　　　and

and so my tongue shall joyfully
    sing of thy righteousnes.
15 O Lord-my-stay, let thou my lips
    by thee be opened,
    and by my mouth thy prayses shall
    be openly shewed.
16 For thou desir'st not sacrifice,
    it would I freely bring:
    neither dost thou contentment take
    in a whole burnt offring.
17 The sacrifices of the Lord
    they are a broken sprite:
    God, thou wilt not despise a heart
    that's broken, & contrite.
13 In thy good pleasure o doe thou
    doe good to Sion hill:
    the walles of thy Ierusalem
    o doe thou build up still.
19 The sacrifice of justice shall
    please thee, with burnt offring,
    and whole burnt offring; then they shall
    calves to thine Altar bring.

Another of the same.

O GOD, have mercy upon mee,
    according to thy kindenes deare:
and as thy mercyes many bee,
    quite doe thou my transgressions cleare.
2   From my perversues mee wash through,
    and from my sin mee purify.
3 For my transgressions I doe know,

before

before mee is my fin dayly.

4   Gainft thee,thee only fin'd have I,
    & done this evill in thy fight:
    that when thou fpeakft thee juftify
    men may,and judging cleare thee quite.

5   Loe,in injuftice fhape't I was:
    in fin my mother conceav'd mee.

6   Loe,thou in th'inwards truth lov'd haz:
    and made mee wife in fecrecie.

7   Purge me with hyffope,& I cleare
    fhall be;mee wafh,& then the fnow

8   I fhall be whiter. Make me heare
    Ioy & gladnes, the bones which fo
      Thou broken haft joy cheerly fhall.

9   Hyde from my fins thy face away
    blot thou iniquityes out all
    which are upon mee any way.

           (2)

10   Create in mee cleane heart *at laft*
    God: a right fpirit in me new make.

11   Nor from thy prefence quite me caft,
    thy holy fpright nor from me take.

12   Mee thy falvations joy reftore,
    and ftay me with thy fpirit free.

13   I wil, tranfgreffors teach thy lore,
    and finners fhall be turnd to thee.

14   Deliver mee from guilt of bloud,
    o God, God of my health-faving,
    which if thou fhalt vouchfafe,aloud
    thy righteoufnes my tongue fhall fing.

15   My lips doe thou,o Lord,unclofe,

               and

and thy prayse shall my mouth forth show.

16 For sacrifice thou hast not chose,
   that I should it on thee bestow:
     Thou joy'st not in burnt sacrifice.

17 Gods sacrifices are a sp'ryte
   broken; o God, thou'lt not despise,
   a heart that's broken & contrite.

18   In thy good will doe thou bestow
   on Sion goodnes bounteouslie:
   Ierusalems walles that lye so low
   doe thou vouchsafe to edifie.

19   Then shalt thou please to entertaine
   the sacrifices with content
   of righteousnes, the offrings slaine,
   which unto thee wee shall present,
     Together with the offerings
   such as in fire whole burned are:
   and then they shall their bullocks bring,
   offrings to be on thine altar.

Psalme 52

To the chief musician, *Maschil*. a psalme of
   David: when Doeg the Edomite came and
   told Saule, & sayd unto him, Dauid is
   come to the house of Ahimilech.

O Man of might, wherefore dost thou
   thus boast thy selfe in ill?
the goodnes of the mighty God
   endureth ever still.

2 Thy tongue presumptuously doth
   mischievous things devise:
   it is like to a razor sharp,

                     working

working deceitfull lies.

3 Thou loveſt evil more then good,
    more to ſpeak lies then right.

4 O guilefull tongue, thou doſt in all
    devouring words delight.

5 God ſhall likewiſe for evermore
    deſtroying thee deface,
he ſhall take thee away, & pluck
    thee from thy dwelling place,
And alſo root thee out from off
    the land of the living.   Selah.

6 The righteous alſo ſhall it ſee
    and feare, at him laughing.

7 Loe, this the man *that* made not God
    his ſtrength: but truſted in
his ſtore of wealth, himſelfe made ſtrong
    in his miſchievous ſin.

8 But in the houſe of God *am* I
    like a greene Olive-tree:
I truſt for ever & for aye,
    in Gods benignitie.

9 Thee will I prayſe for evermore,
    becauſe thou haſt done this:
and I'le wayt on thy name, for good
    before thy Saints that is.

Pſalme 53.

To the chief muſician upon Mahalath,
    Maſchil. a *pſalme* of David.

THe foole in's heart ſaith, *there's* no God;
    they are corrupt, have done
abominable practiſes;

that doth good there is none.
2 The Lord from heaven looked downe
   on fonnes of men, to fee
if any that doth underftand,
   that feeketh God there bee.
3 All are gone back,together they
   ev'n filthy are become:
and there is none that doeth good,
   noe not fo much as one.
4 The workers of iniquityes
   have they noe knowledge all?
who eate my people: they eate bread;
   and on God doe not call.
5 Greatly they fear'd,*where* noe feare was,
   'gainft thee in camp that lyes
his bones God fcattered;& them fham'd
   for God doth *them* defpife.
6 Who Ifraells health from Sion gives?
   his folks captivitie
when God fhall turne: Iacob fhall joye
   glad Ifraell fhall bee.

Pfalme 54

To the chief mufician on Neginoth,Mafchil,*a*
pfalm: of David,when the Ziphims came & fayd
to Saul,doth not David hide himfelfe with us?

PReferve mee,by thy name,o God,
   & by thy ftrength judge mee.
2 O God,my pray'r heare,give eare to
   words in my mouth that bee.
3 For ftrangers up againft me rife,
   and who oppreffe me fore,

                                        purfue

purfue my foule;neither have they
    fet God themfelves before.   Selah.
4 Loe, God helps mee,the Lord's with them
    that doe my foule fuftaine.
5 He fhall reward ill to my foes:
    them in thy truth reftrayne.
6 Vnto thee facrifice will I,
    with voluntarines;
Lord,to thy name I will give prayfe,
    becaufe of thy goodnes.
7 For he hath mee delivered,
    out of all miferyes:
and i.s defire mine eye hath feen
    upon mine enemyes.

Pfalme 55

To the chief mufician on Neginoth,Mafchil,
    a pfalme of David.

O GOD,doe thou give eare unto
    my fupplication:
and doe not hide thy felfe away
    from my petition.
2 Bee thou attentive unto mee,
    and anfwer mee returne,
I in my meditation
    doe make a noyfe & mourne.
3 Becaufe of th'enemies voyce,becaufe
    the wicked haue oppreft,
for they injuftice on mee caft
    and in wrath mee deteft.
4 My heart in mee is payn'd,on mee
    deaths terrors fallen bee.

                5 Trembling

5 Trembling & feare are on mee come,
   horrour hath covered mee.
6 Then did I fay, o who to mee
   wings of a dove will give;
   that I might flie away & might
   in quiet dwelling live.
7 *Loe*, I would wander farre away,
   and in the defart reft.   Selah,
8 Soone would I fcape from windy ftorme,
   from violent tempeft.

(2)

9 Lord bring on them deftruction,
   doe thou their tongues divide;
   for ftrife & violence I within
   the city have efpy'd.
10 About it on the walles thereof,
   they doe walk night & day:
   mifchief alfo & forrow doe
   in middeft of it ftay.
11 In midft thereof there's wickednes;
   deceitfullnes alfo,
   and out of the broad ftreets thereof
   guilefullnes doth not go.
12 For t'was no foe reproacht mee, then
   could I have borne; nor did
   my foe againft me lift himfelfe
   from him had I me hid.
13 But thou it was, the man that wert
   my well efteemed peere,
   which waft to mee my fpeciall guide,
   and mine acquaintance neere.

14 wee

14 Wee did together counsell take
    in sweet society:
and wee did walk into the house
    of God in company.

15 Let death seize on them,& let them
    goe downe quick into hell:
for wickednes among them is
    in places where they dwell.

(2)

16 As for mee, I will call on God;
    and mee the Lord save shall.

17 Ev'ning morn,& at noon will I
    pray, & aloud will call,

18 and he shall heare my voyce. He hath
    in peace my soule set free
from warre that was 'gainst mee,because
    there many were with mee.

19 God shall heare,& them smite,ev'n he
    that doth of old abide;   Selah.
because they have no change,therefore
    Gods feare they lay aside.

20 Gainst such as be at peace with him
    hee hath put forth his hand:
he hath also the covenant
    which he had made prophan'd.

21 His words then butter smoother were,
    but warre in's heart:his words
more then the oyle were softened
    but yet they were drawne swords.

22 Thy burden cast upon the Lord,
    and he sustaine thee shall:

nor

nor ſhall he ſuffer righteous ones
    to be remov'd at all.
23 But thou o God,ſhalt downe to hell
    bring them who bloody bee,
  guilefull ſhall not live halfe their dayes:
    but I will truſt in thee.

Pſalme 56.

To the chief muſician upō Ionath Elem Recho-
-kim,Michtam of David,when the Philiſtims
            tooke him ın Gath.

L ORD, pitty mee,becauſe
    man would up ſwallow mee:
  and fighting all the day throughout,
    oppreſſe mee ſore doth hee.
2 Mine enemies they would
    me ſwallow up dayly;
  for they *be* many that doe fight
    againſt mee,o moſt high.
3 I'le put my truſt in thee,
    what time I am afrayd.
4 In God I'le prayſe his word,in God
    my confidence have ſtayd;
  I will not be afrayd
    what fleſh can doe to mee.
5 All day they wreſt my words:their thoughts
    for ill againſt me bee.
6 They joyne themſeves together;
    themſelves they cloſely hyde;
  they mark my ſteps when for my ſoule
    wayting they doe abyde.
7 Shall they make an eſcape

                                    by

by their iniquity;
   thou in thine anger downe depreſſe
     the folk, o God mighty.
8 My wandrings thou doſt tell,
     put thou my weeping teares
   into thy bottle; *are* they not
     within thy regiſters.
9 Then ſhall my foes turne back,
     when I crye unto thee:
   this I doe know aſſuredly,
     becauſe God is for mee.
10 In God I'le prayſe his word:
     the Lords word I will prayſe.
11 In God I truſt:I will not feare
     what man 'gainſt mee can rayſe.
12 Thy vowes on me o God,
     I'le render prayſe to thee.
13 Becauſe that thou my ſoule from death
     delivering doſt free;
   Deliver wilt not thou
     my feet from downe falling?
   ſo that I may walk before God
     ith light of the living.

Pſalme 57

To the chief muſician Altaſchith, Michtam of
   David,when he fled from Saul in the cave.

O GOD,to me be mercifull,
     be mercifull to mee:
   becauſe my ſoule for ſhelter-ſaſe
     betakes it ſelfe to thee.
Yea in the ſhaddow of thy wings,
     my refuge I have plac't,   N 2   untill

untill thefe fore calamities
  shall quite be over past.

2 To God most high I cry:the God
  that doth for me performe.

3 He will from heaven fend, & fave
  mee from the fpightfull fcorne
Of him that would with greedy haft,
  fwallow me vtterly: Selah.
the Lord from heaven will fend forth
  his grace & verity.

4 My foule's 'mongft lions, & I lye
  with men on-fier-fet:
mens fonnes whofe teeth are fpears,& fhafts,
  whofe tongues as fwords are whet.

5 O God,doe thou exalt thy felfe,
  above the heavens high:
up over all the earth alfo
  lifted be thy glory.

6 They for my fteps prepar'd a net,
  my foule is bow'd; a pit
they dig'd before me, but *themfelves*
  are fall'n in midft of it.   Selah.

7 My heart o God, prepared is,
  prepared is my heart,
fing will I, & fing prayfe with pfalmes.

8   Vp o my glorie ftart;
Wake Pfaltery & Harp, I will
  awake in the morning.

9 Among the folk I'le prayfe thee,Lord,
  'mongft nations to thee fing.

10 For great unto the heavens is
     thy mercifull bounty:
  thy verity alſo doth reach
     unto the cloudy ſkye.
11 O God, doe thou exalt thy ſelfe,
     above the heavens high:
  up over all the earth alſo
     lifted *be* thy glory.

Pſalme 5 8

To the chief muſician, Altaſchiːh,
     michtam of David.

DOe yee o congregation,
     indeed ſpeak righteouſnes?
  and o yee ſons of earthly men,
     doe yee judge uprightnes?
2 Yea you in heart will working be
     injurious-wickednes;
  and in the land you will weigh out
     your hands violentnes.
3 The wicked are eſtranged from
     the womb, they goe aſtray
  as ſoone as ever they are borne;
     uttering lyes are they.
4 Their poyſon's like ſerpents poyſon:
     they like deafe Aſpe, her eare
5 that ſtops. Though Charmer wiſely charme,
     his voice ſhe will not heare.
6 Within their mouth doe thou their teeth
     break out, o God moſt ſtrong,
  doe thou Iehovah, the great teeth
     break of the lions young.

N 3   7 As

7 As waters let them melt away,
    that run continually:
and when he bends his shafts, let them
    as cut asunder bee.

8 Like to a snayle that melts, so let
    each of them passe away;
like to a womans untimely birth
    see Sun that neuer they may.

9 Before your potts can feele the thornes,
    take them away shall hee,
as with a whirlwinde both living,
    and in his jealousee.

10 The righteous will rejoyce when as
    the vengeance he doth see:
his feet wash shall he in the blood
    of them that wicked bee.

11 So that a man shall say, surely
    for righteous there is fruit:
sure there's a God that in the earth
    judgement doth execute.

Psalme 59

To the chief musician Altaschith, Michtam of
David:when Saul sent, & they watched the
house to kill him.

O GOD from them deliver mee
    that are mine enemies:
set thou me up on high from them
    that up against me rise.

2 Deliver mee from them that work
    grievous-iniquity:
and be a saviour unto mee

from

from men that be bloody.

3 For loe,they for my foule lay wayt;
   the ftrong caufleffe combine
against me,not for my crime,Lord,
   nor any fin of mine.

4 Without iniquity in me
   they run, & ready make
themfelves,doe thou behold,alfo
   unto my help awake.

5 Lord God of hoaft,thou Ifraels God,
   rife to vifit therefore
all heathens;who fin wilfully,
   to them fhew grace no more.

6 At ev'ning they returne,& like
   to dogs a noyfe doe make;
and fo about the city round
   a compaffe they doe take.

7 Behold they belch out with their mouths,
   within their lips fwords are:
for who is he (doe thefe men fay)
   which *us* at all doth heare.

8 But thou o *L*ord,at them wilt laugh,
   and heathens all wilt mock.

9 *And for* his ftrength. I'le wayt on thee
   for God is my high Rock.
            (2)

10 God of my mercy manyfold
   with good fhall prevent mee:
and my defire upon my foes
   the Lord will let mee fee.

11 Slay them not,left my folk forget:

                              but

    but scatter them abroad
  by thy strong-power;& bring them downe,
    who art our shield o God.

12 For their mouths sin,& their lips words,
    and in their pride them take:
  and for their cursing,& lying
    which in their speech they make.

13 Consume in wrath, consume & let
    them be no more;that they
  may know that God in Iacob rules,
    to th'ends of th'earth. Selah.

14 And at ev'ning let them returne,
    and like dogs a noyse make;
  and so about the citty round
    a compasse let them take.

15 And let them wander up & downe
    seeking what they may eat,
  and if they be not satissiyde,
    then let them grudge thereat.

16 But I will sing thy powre;& shout
    i'th morning thy kindenesse:
  for thou my towre & refuge art
    in day of my distresse.

17 Thou art my strength,& unto thee,
    sing psalmes of prayse will I:
  for God is mine high towre, he is
    the God of my mercy.

Psalme 60.

To the chief musician upon Shushan Eduth
Michtam of David,to teach. when he strove with
Aram Naharaim, & with Aram Zobah when
                          Ioab

PSALME lx.

Ioab returned,& smote of Edom in the valley
of salt, twelve thousand.

O GOD, thou hast rejected us,
   and scattered us abroad:
thou hast displeased been with us,
   returne to us o God.

2 The land to tremble thou hast caus'd,
   thou it asunder brake:
doe thou the breaches of it heale,
   for it doth moveing shake.

3 Thou hast unto thy people shew'd
   things that are hard, thou hast
also the cup of trembleing
   given to them to tast.

4 But unto them that doe thee feare,
   a Banner to display
thou given hast to be lift up
   for thy truths sake.Selah.

5 That those who thy beloved are
   delivered may bee,
o doe thou save with thy right hand,
   and answer give to mee.

6 God in his holynes hath spoke,
   rejoyce therein will I,
Shechem I will divide,& meete
   of Succoth the valley.

7 To mee doth Gilead appertaine,
   Manasseh mine besides:
Ephraim the strength is of my head,
   Iudah my lawes prescribes.

8 Moab's my wash-pot, I will cast

over Edom my shoo,
  o Palestine, because of mee
  be thou triumphant too.
9 O who is it that will mee lead
  to th'citty fortifyde?
  and who is he that will become
  into Edom my guide?
10 Is it not thou,o God,who hadst
  cast us off heretofore?
  and thou o God,who with our hoasts
  wouldst not goe out before?
11 O give to us help from distresse
  for mans help is but vaine:
12 Through God wee'l doe great acts,he shall
  our foes tread with disdaine.

Psalme 61

To the chief musician upon Neginath,
A psalme of David.

HArken o God, unto my cry,
  unto my prayr attend.
2 When my heart is opprest, I'le cry
  to thee from the earths end.
  Doe thou mee lead unto the rock
  that higher is then I.
3 For thou my hiding-place, hast been
  strong Fort from th'enemy.
4 Within thy Tabernacle I
  for ever will abide,
  within the covert of thy wings
  I'le seek my selfe to hide.   Selah·
5 For thou o God,hast heard the vowes

that

that I to thee have paſt:
their heritage that feare thy name
  to mee thou given haſt.
6 Thou to the dayes of the Kings life
    wilt make addition:
his yeares as generation,
  and generation.
7 Before the face of the ſtrong God
    he ſhall abide for aye:
doe thou mercy & truth prepare
  that him preſerve they may.
8 So then I will unto thy name
    ſing prayſe perpetually,
that I the vowes which I have made
  may pay continually.

Pſalme 62
To the chief muſician, to Ieduthun,
a pſalme of David.

TRuly my ſoule in ſilence waytes
  the mighty God upon:
from him it is that there doth come
  all my ſalvation.
2 He only is my rock, & my
    ſalvation; it is hee
that my defence is, ſo that I
  mov'd greatly ſhall not bee.
3 How long will yee miſchief deviſe
    'gainſt man; be ſlaine yee ſhall,
all yee are as a rottring fence,
  & like a bowing wall.
4 Yet they conſult to caſt him downe

O 2

from

from his excellency:
lyes they doe love, with mouth they bleſſe,
    but they curſe inwardly.   Selah.
5 Yet thou my ſoule in ſilent wayt
    the mighty God upon:
because from him there doth ariſe
    my expectation.
6 He only is my rock, & my
    ſalvation; it is hee
that my defence is, ſo that I
    ſhall never mooved bee.
7 In God is my ſalvation,
    alſo is my glory:
and the rock of my fortitude,
    my hope in God doth ly.
8 Yee people, ſee that you on him
    doe put your truſt alway,
before him poure ye out your hearts:
    God is our hopefull-ſtay.   Selah.
9 Surely meane men are vanity
    high mens ſonnes are a lye:
in ballance laid together are
    lighter then vanity.
10 In robbery be not vaine, truſt not
    yee in oppreſſion:
if ſo be riches doe increaſe
    ſet not your heart *thereon.*
11 The mighty God hath ſpoken once:
    once & againe this word
I have it heard that *all* power
    belongs unto the Lord.

12 Alſo

12 Alſo to thee benignity
  o Lord, doth *appertaine*:
for thou according to his work
  rendreſt each man againe.

Pſalme 63

A pſalme of David, when he was in the
  wildernes of Iudah.

O GOD, thou art my God, early
  I will for thee inquire:
my ſoule thirſteth for thee, my fleſh
  for thee hath ſtrong deſire,
In land whereas no water is
  that thirſty is & dry.
2 To ſee, as I ſaw in thine houſe
  thy ſtrength & thy glory.
3 Becauſe thy loving kindenes doth
  abundantly excell
ev'n life it ſelfe: wherefore my lips
  forth ſhall thy prayſes tell.
4 Thus will I bleſſing give to thee
  whilſt that alive am I:
and in thy name I will lift up
  theſe hands of mine on high.
5 My ſoule as with marrow & fat
  ſhall ſatiſfied bee:
my mouth alſo with joyfull lips
  ſhall prayſe give unto thee.
6 When as that I remembrance have
  of thee my bed upon,
and on thee in the night watches
  have meditation.

O 3   7 Be-

7 Becaufe that thou haft been to me
    he that to me help brings;
 therefore will I fing joyfully
    in fhaddow of thy wings.
8 My foule out of an ardent love
    doth follow after thee:
 alfo thy right hand it is that
    which hath upholden mee.
9 But as for thofe that feek my foule
    to bring it to an end,
 they fhall into the lower parts
    of the earth downe defcend.
10 By the hand of the fword alfo
    they fhall be made to fall:
 and they be for a portion
    unto the Foxes fhall.
11 But the King fhall rejoyce in **God**,
    all that by him doe fweare
 fhall glory, but ftopped fhall be
    their mouths that lyars are.

Pfalme 64
To the chief mufician, a pfalme
of David.

O GOD, when I my prayer make,
    my voyce *then* doe thou heare;
 alfo doe thou preferve my life
    fafe from the enemies feare.
2 And from the fecret counfell of
    the wicked hide thou mee:
 from th' infurection of them
    that work iniquitee.

3 who

PSALME lxiv.

3 Who have their tongue now sharpened
  like as it were a sword;
and bend *their bowes to shoot* their shafts
  ev'n a most bitter word:
4 That they in secrecie may shoot
  the perfect man to hitt.
suddenly doe they shoot at him,
  & never feare a whitt.
5 Them selves they in a matter ill
  encourage; how they may
lay snares in secret, thus they talk;
  who shall them see? they say.
6 They doe search out iniquity,
  a search exact they keep:
both inward thought of euery man
  also the heart is deep.
7 But God shall shoot at them a shaft,
  be sudden their wound shall.
8 So that they shall make their owne tongue
  upon themselves to fall,
All that see them shall flee away.
9 All men shall feare, & tell
the works of God, for his doeing
  they shall consider well.
10 The just shall in the Lord be glad,
  and trust in him he shall:
and they that upright are in heart
  in him shall glory all.
              Psalme 65
      To the chief musician, a psalme and
          song of David.
                      PSALM

O GOD, in Sion silently
    prayfe wayteth upon thee:
  and thankfully unto thee fhall
    the vow performed bee.
2 O thou that harken doft unto
    the prayr that men doe make,
  ev'n unto thee therefore all flefh
    themfelves they fhall betake.
3 Works of iniquitie they have
    prevailed againft mee;
  as for our trefpaffes they fhall
    be purgde away by thee.
4 O bleffed is the man of whom
    thou thy free choyce doft make;
  and that he may dwell in thy courts
    him neere to thee doft take:
  For with the good things of thy houfe
    be fatiffyde fhall wee;
  and with the holy things likwife
    that in thy temple bee.
5 In righteoufnes, thou, by the things
    that dreadfully are done,
  wilt anfwer give to us, o God,
    of our falvation:
  Vpon whom all the ends of th'earth
    do confidently ftay,
  & likewife they that are remov'd
    far off upon the fea.
6 He fes faft mountaines by his ftrength
7   girt with might. Hee doth fwage
  the noyfe of feas, noyfe of their waves

                                    alfo

also the peoples rage.

(2)

8 They at thy tokens are afrayd
　　that dwell in parts far out;
　out goings of the morning thou
　　and ev'ning makſt to ſhout.
9 Thou viſiteſt the earth,& doſt
　　it moiſten plenteouſly,
　thou with Gods ſtreame,full of water
　　enricheſt it greatly:
　When thou haſt ſo prepared ir,
　　thou doſt them corne prepare.
10　The ridges thou abundantly
　　watreſt that in it are;
　The furrows of it thou ſetleſt,
　　with ſhowers that do fall
　thou makſt it ſoft,thou doſt therof
　　the ſpringing bleſſe withall.
11 Thou doſt the yeare with thy goodnes
　　adorne as with a crowne,
　alſo the paths where thou doſt tread,
　　fatnes they doe drop downe.
12 They drop upon the paſtures that
　　are in the wildernes;
　and girded are the little hills
　　about with joyfullnes.
13　Clothed the paſtures are with flocks,
　　corne over-covering
　the valleys is;ſo that for joy
　　they ſhout, they alſo ſing.

P

Pſalme **66**

To the chief muſician a pſalme or ſong.

O All yee lands, a joyfull noyſe
   unto God doe yee rayſe.

2 Sing forth the honour of his name:
   make glorious his prayſe.

3 How dreadfull in thy works art thou?
   unto the Lord ſay yee:
through thy powres greatnes thy foes ſhall
   ſubmit themſelves to thee.

4 All they ſhall bow themſelves to thee
   that dwell upon the earth,
and ſing unto thee, they ſhall ſing
   unto thy name with mirth.   Selah.

5 Come hither, alſo of the works
   of God take yee notice,
he in his doing terrible
   towards mens children is.

6 He did the ſea into dry land
   convert, a way they had
on foot to paſſe the river through,
   there we in him were glad.

7 He ruleth by his powre for ever,
   his eyes the nations ſpie:
let not thoſe that rebellious are
   lift up themſelves on high.   Selah.

8 Yee people bleſſe our God, & make   (2 *part*)
   his prayſes voyce be heard.

9 Which holds our ſoule in life, our feet
   nor ſuffers to be ſtird.

10 For God thou haſt us prov'd, thou haſt

us tryde as filver's tryde.
11 Into the net brought us,thou haft
on our loynes ftreightnes tyde.
12 Men o're our heads thou madft to ride,
through fire & water paffe
did wee,but us thou broughft into
a place that wealthy was.
13 With offrings I'le go to thine houfe:
my vowes I'le pay to thee.
14 Which my lips uttred, & mouth fpake,
when trouble was on mee.
15 Burnt offrings I'le offer to thee
that full of fatnes are,
with the incenfe of rams,I will
bullocks with goates prepare.   Selah.
16 Come harken unto me all yee   (3 part)
of God that fearers are,
and what he hath done for my foule
to you I will declare.
17 With mouth I cryde to him, & with
my tongue extoll'd was hee.
18 If in my heart I fin regard
the Lord will not heare mee.
19 But God that is moft mighty hath
me heard affuredly;
unto the voyce of my prayr he
lift'ned-attentively.
20 Bleft be the mighty God,becaufe
neither my prayr hath hee,
nor yet his owne benignity,
turned away from mee.

Pſalme 67

To the chief muſician on Neginoth
a pſalme *or* Song.

GOD gracious be to us,& give
his bleſſing us unto,
let him upon us make to ſhine
his countenance alſo.   Selah.

2 That there may be the knowledg of
thy way the earth upon,
and alſo of thy ſaving health
in every nation.

3 O God let thee the people prayſe,
let all people prayſe thee.

4 O let the nations rejoyce,
and let them joyfull bee:
For thou ſhalt give judgement unto
the people righteouſly,
alſo the nations upon earth
thou ſhalt them lead ſafely.   Selah.

5 O God let thee the people prayſe
let all people prayſe thee.

6 *Her* fruitfull increaſe by the earth
ſhall then forth yeilded bee:
God ev'n our owne God ſhall us bleſſe.

7   God *I ſay* bleſſe us ſhall,
and of the earth the utmoſt coaſts
they ſhall him reverence all.

Pſalme 68

To the chief muſician, a pſalme or ſong
of David.

psalme

PSALME lxviii.

L Et God arise, his enemies
  let them difperfed bee,
    let them alfo that doe him hate
      away from his face flee.
2 As fmoake is driven away, ev'n fo
    doe thou them drive away:
  as wax at fire melts, in Gods fight
    let wicked fo decay.
3 But let the righteous ones be glad:
    o let them joyfull bee
  before the Lord, alfo let them
    rejoyce exceedinglie.
4 Sing to God, to his name fing prayfe,
    extoll him that doth ride
  on fkies, by his name I AH, before
    his face joyfull abide.
5 A father of the fatherleffe,
    and of the widdows cafe
  God is a judge, & that within
    his holy dwelling place.
6 God feates the defolate in houfe,
    brings forth thofe that are bound
  in chaines, but the rebellious
    dwell in a barren ground.
(2)
7 O God when as thou didft goe forth
    in prefence of thy folk,
  when through the defart wildernes
    thou diddeft marching walk.   Selah.
8 The earth did at Gods prefence fhake,
    from heav'ns the drops downe fell:

Sinai it selfe moved before

    the God of Israell.

9 O God thou on thy heritage
    didst send a plenteous raine,
 whereby when as it weary was
    thou it confirm'd againe.

10 Thy congregation hath dwelt
    therin, thou dost prepare
 o God of thy goodnes, for them
    that poore afflicted are.

11 The Lord the word gave, great their troup
    that it have published.

12 Kings of hoasts fled, fled, she that stayd
    at home spoyle devided.

13 Though yee have lyen among the pots,
    be like doves wings shall yee
 with silver deckt, & her feathers
    like yellow gold that bee.

14 When there th'Almighty scattred Kings,
    t'was white as Salmons snow.

15 Gods hill like Bashan hill, high hill,
    like Bashan hill unto.

16 Why doe ye leap ye lofty hills?
    this is the very hill
 in which God loves to dwell, the Lord
    dwell in it ever will.

(3)

17 Gods charrets twice ten thousand fold,
    thousands of Angells bee;
 with them as in his holy place,
    on Sinai mount is hee.

18 Thou didst ascend on high, thou ledst
    captivity captive,

                        for

for men, yea, for rebells alſo
  thou diddeſt gifts receive;
That the Lord God might dwell with them.
19 *Who* dayly doth us load
  with benefits, bleſt be the Lord
    that's our ſalvations God.   Selah.
20 He is God of ſalvation
    that is our God moſt ſtrong:
  and unto Iehovah the Lord
    iſſues from death belong.
21 But God ſhall wound the enemies head,
    the hairy ſcalp alſo
  of him that in his treſpaſſes
    on forward ſtill doth go.
           (4)
22 The Lord ſayd I·le bring back againe,
    againe from Baſhan hill:
  my people from the depths of ſeas
    bring back againe I will.
23 That thy foot may be dipt within
    blood of thine enemyes;
  imbrude the tongue of thy dogs may
    be in the ſame likewyſe.
24 They have thy goings ſeene o God
    thy goings in progreſſe;
  ev'n of my God my King within
    place of his holyneſſe.
25 Singers went firſt, muſicians then,
    in midſt maids with Timbrel.
26 Bleſſe God i'th Churches, the Lord from
    the ſpring of Iſraell.
27 There litle Benjamin the chief
    with Iudahs Lords,& their   counſel

PSALM lxviii.

counsell, with Zebulons princes,
and Naphtalies lords were.
23 That valliant strength the which thou haft
thy God hath commanded,
ftrengthen o God, the thing which thou
for us haft effected.

(4)

29 For thy houfe at Ierufalem
Kings fhall bring gifts to thee.
30 Rebuke the troups of fpearmen, troups
of bulls that mighty bee:
With peoples calves, with him that ftoops
with peeces of filvar:
o fcatter thou the people that
delight themfelves in war.
31 Princes fhall out of Egipt come,
& Ethiopias land
fhall fpeedily unto the Lord
reach her out-ftreched hand.
32 Earths kingdomes fing yee unto God:
unto the Lord fing prayfe.   Selah.
33 To him that rides on heav'ns of heav'ns
that were of ancient dayes:
Loe, he his voyce, a ftrong voyce gives.
34   To God afcribe yee might,
his excellence o're Ifraell is,
& his ftrength in the height.
35 God fearfull from his holy place
the God of Ifraell, hee
gives ftrength & powre unto his folk,
o let God bleffed bee.

psalme

PSALME lxix.

To the chief muſician upon Shoſhannim,
A pſalme of David.

THe waters in unto my ſoule
    are come, o God, me ſave.
2 I am in muddy deep ſunk downe,
    where I no ſtanding have:
Into deep waters I am come,
    where floods mee overflow.
3 I of my crying weary am,
    my throat is dryed ſo;
Mine eyes faile: I wayt for my God.
4   They that have hated mee
without a cauſe, then mine heads haires
    they more in number bee:
Alſo mine enemies wrongfully
    they are that would me ſlay,
mighty they are; then I reſtor'd
    what I took not away.
5 O God thou knowſt my fooliſhnes;
    my ſin's not hid from thee.
6 Who wayt on thee, Lord God of hoaſts,
    let not be ſhamd for mee:
O never ſuffer them, who doe
    for thee inquiry make,
o God of Iſraell, to be
    confounded for my ſake,

(2)

7 By reaſon that I for thy ſake,
    reproach have ſuffered:
confuſion my countenance
    hath overcovered.

Q

8 I as a stranger am become
    unto my bretherren;
and am an aliant unto
    my mothers childerren.

9 For of thy house the zeale me hath
    up eaten: every one
who thee reproach, their reproaches
    are fallen mee upon

10 In fasts, I wept & spent my soule,
    this was reproach to mee.

11 And I my garment sackcloth made:
    yet must their proverb bee.

12 They that do sit within the gate,
    against mee speak they do;
unto the drinkers of strong drink,
    I was a song also.

13 But I in an accepted time
    to thee Lord, make my prayr:
mee Lord, in thy salvations truth,
    in thy great mercy heare.

(3)

14 Deliver me out of the mire,
    and mee from sinking keep:
let mee be freed mine haters from,
    and out of waters deep.

15 O'reflow mee let not water floods,
    nor mee let swallow up
the deep, also let not the pitt
    her mouth upon mee shut.

16 Iehovah heare thou mee, for good
    is thy benignity:

turne

PSALME lxix.

turne unto mee according to
   greatnes of thy mercy.
17 And hide not thou thy countenance
   from thy servant away;
   because that I in trouble am;
   heare me without delay.
18 O draw thou nigh unto my soule,
   doe thou it vindicate;
   give mee deliverance, because
   of them that doe mee hate.
19 Thou hast knowne my reproach, also
   my shame, & my disgrace:
   mine adversaryes every one
   they are before thy face.
(4)
20 Reproach mine heart brake, I was griev'd:
   for some me to bemone
   I sought, but none there was; & for
   comforters, but found none.
21 Moreover in stead of my meate
   unto mee gall they gave;
   and in me thirst they vineger
   for drink made me to have.
22 Their table set before their face,
   to them become a snare:
   and *that let be* a trap, *which should
   have been* for *their* welfare.
23 And let their eyes be darkened,
   that they may never see:
   their loynes also with trembleing
   to shake continuallee.

Q 2   24 Poure

24 Poure out thine ire on them, let feize
   on them thine anger fell.

25 Their Pallace let be defolate:
   none in their tents let dwell.

26 Becaufe they *him* doe perfecute
   on whom thy ftroke is found:
  alfo they talk unto the grief
   of them whom thou doft wound.

27 Thou unto their iniquity
   iniquity doe add:
  into thy righteoufnes for them
   let entrance none be had.

28 Out of the book of the living
   o doe thou them forth blot,
  and amongft them that righteous are
   be written let them not.

(5)

29 But Lord, I'me poore & forrowfull:
   let thy health lift me hy.

30 With fong I'le prayfe the name of God:
   with thanks him magnify.

31 Vnto Iehovah *this* alfo
   fhall be more pleafing far,
  then *any* oxe *or* bullock young,
   that horn'd & hoofed are.

32 This thing when as they fhall behold,
   then fhall be glad the meek;
  alfo their heart fhall ever live
   that after God doe feek.

33 For the Lord hears the poore, nor doth
   defpife whom he hath bound.

34 Let

34 Let heav'n,earth, feas & all therin
    that moves, his prayfes found.

35 For God will Iudahs cittyes build,
    and Sion he will fave:
  that they may dwell therin,& may
    it in poffeffion have.

36 The feed alfo of his fervants
    inherit fhall the fame:
  alfo therin inhabit fhall
    they that doe love his name.

Pfalme 70

To the chief mufician, a pfalme to bring
    to remembrance.

O GOD, to refcue mee,
    Lord,to mine help,make haft.

2 Let them that after my foule feek
    afham'd be, & abafht:
  Turnd back & fhamd let them
    that in my hurt delight.

3 Turnd back let them ha, ha, that fay,
    their fhame for to requite.

4 Let all thofe that thee feek
    joy, & be glad in thee:
  let fuch as love thy health fay ftill,
    magnifyde let God bee.

5 Make haft to me Lord, for
    I poore am & needy:
  thou art mine ayd, & my helper
    o Lord; doe not tarry.

Pfalme 71

R 3   PSALM

PSALM lxxi.

IEHOVAH, I for safety doe
  betake my selfe to thee:
o let me not at any time
  put to confusion bee.

2 Me rescue in thy righteousnes,
  let me deliverance have:
to me doe thou incline thine eare,
  also doe thou me save.

3 Be thou my dwelling Rock, whereto
  I alwayes may resort:
thou gav'st commandment me to save,
  for thou my Rock & Fort.

4 Out of the hand of the wicked
  my God, deliver mee,
out of the hand of the unjust,
  leaven'd with crueltie.

5 For thou o God, Iehovah art
  mine expectation:
and thou art hee whom from my youth
  my trust is set upon :

6 Thou hast upheld mee from the womb,
  thou art he that tookst mee
out of my mothers belly; still
  my prayse shall be of thee.

(2)

7 To many I a wonder am
  but thou my refuge strong.

8 Let my mouth fill'd be with thy prayse,
  & honour all day long.

9 Within the time of elder age
  o cast me not away,

and

and doe not thou abandon me
    when my ſtrength doth decay.
10 Becauſe they that be enemyes
    to me, againſt me ſpake,
and they that for my ſoule lay-wayt,
    counſell together take.
11 Saying, God hath forgotten him:
    doe yee him now purſue,
and apprehend him, for *there is*
    not one him to reſcue.
12 Depart not farre from mee, o God,
    my God haſt to helpe mee.
13 The adverſaryes of my ſoule,
    let them aſhamed bee:
Let them conſumed be, let them
    be alſo covered,
both with reproach & diſhonour,
    that for my hurt wayted.
        (3)
14 But *I* with patience will wayt
    on thee continuallee,
and I will adde yet more & more
    to all the prayſe of thee.
15 My mouth it ſhall thy righteouſnes,
    and thy ſalvation ſhow
from day to day, for *of the ſame*
    no number doe I know.
16 In the ſtrong might of God the Lord
    goe on a long will I:
I'le mention make of thy juſtice,
    yea ev'n of thine only.
                  17 fro.n

PSALM lxxi.

17 From my youth up o mighty God,
   thou haſt inſtructed mee:
and hitherto I have declar'd
   the wonders wrought by thee.
18 And now unto mine elder age,
   and hoary head, o God,
doe not forſake mee: till I have
   thy power ſhowne abroad,
Vnto this generation,
   and unto every one
that ſhall hereafter be to come,
   thy ſtrong dominion.
(4)
19 Thy righteouſnes o God, it doth
• reach up on high alſo,
great are the things which thou haſt done;
   Lord who's like thee unto?
20 Thou who haſt cauſed mee to ſee
   afflictions great & ſore,
ſhalt mee revive, & me againe
   from depths of earth reſtore.
21 Thou ſhalt my greatnes multiply
   & comfort me alwayes.
22 Alſo with tuned Pſaltery
   I will ſhew forth thy prayſe,
O thou my God, I will ſing forth
   to thee mine Harp upon,
thy verity & faithfullnes,
   o Iſraels Holy-one.
23 My lips with ſhouting ſhall rejoyce
   when I ſhall ſing to thee:

my

my foule alfo, which freely thou
    haft brought to liberty.
24 Likewife my tongue fhall utter forth
    thy juftice all day long:
for they confounded are, & brought
    to fhame, that feek my wrong.

       Pfalme 72
     A pfalme for Solomon.

O GOD, thy judgements give the King,
    & thy juftice to the Kings Sonne.
2   He fhall thy folk with juftice judge,
    & to thy poore fee judgement done,
3   The mountaines fhall abundantly
    unto the people bring forth peace:
    the little hills fhall bring the fame,
    by executing righteoufnes.
4   Poore of the people he fhall judge,
    and children of the needy fave;
    & he in pecces fhall break downe
    each one that them oppreffed have.
5   They fhall thee feare, while Sun & moon
    endure through generations all.
6   Like raine on mowne graffe he fhall come:
    as fhowres on earth diftilling-fall.
7   The juft fhall flourifh in his dayes,
    & ftore of peace till no moore bee.
8   And from the fea unto the fea,
    from floud to lands end reigne fhall hee.
9   They that within the wildernes
    doe dwell, before him bow they muft:
    and they who are his enemies

            K   they

they verily shall lick the dust.

(2)

10 Vpon him presents shall bestow
of Tarshish, & the Iles, the Kings,
Shebahs, & Sebahs Kings also,
shall unto him give offerings.
11 Yea to him all the kings shall fall,
& serve him every nation:
12 For needy crying save he shall,
the poore, & helper that hath none.
13 The poore & needy he shall spare,
and the soules of the needy save.
14 Their soules from fraud & violence
by him shall free redemption have:
And pretious in his sight shall be
15 the bloud of them. And he shall live,
and unto him shall *every one*
of purest gold of Shebah give:
Also each one their humble prayr
in his behalfe shall make alwayes:
and every one his blessednes
shall dayly celebrate with prayse.

(3)

16 Of corne an handfull there shall be
ith land the mountains tops upon,
the fruit whereof shall moving shake
like to the trees of Lebanon:
And they that of the citty be
like grasse on earth shall flourish all.
17 His name for ever shall indure
as long as Sun continue shall:

PSALME lxxii.

So shall his name continued be,
and men in him themselves shall blesse,
and all the nations of the world
shall him the blessed one professe.

18   O let Iehovah blessed be,
the God, the God of Israell,
hee worketh by himselfe alone
such things whereat men may marvell.

19   And blessed be his glorious name
for ever, let the whole earth be
fill'd full with glory of the same,
Amen, also Amen *say wee.*

This.   *After the common tunes.*

19 And aye be blest his glorious name,
also let the earth all
be filled with his glorious fame,
Amen, & so it shall.

---

20   **The prayers of David, the
Son of Iesse, are
ended.**

THE
THIRD BOOKE.

Pſalme 73
A pſalme of Aſaph.

TRuly to Iſraell God is good,
    to men of a cleane heart.
2 But my feet almoſt ſlipt, my ſteps
    aſide did well nigh ſtarr.
3 For I was envious at the fooles,
    in peace to ſee the ill.
4 For in their death no ban 's there are,
    but firme their ſtrength is ſtill.
5 Like other meane men they are not
    in toyleſome miſery,
nor are they ſtricken with like plagues
    as other mortals bee.
6 Therefore doth pride like to a chaine
    encompaſſe them about,
and like a garment; violence
    doth cover them throughout.
7 Within the fatnes *which they have*
    extended are their eyes:
greater proſperity they have
    then their hearts can deviſe.
8 Corrupt they are, & wickedly
    ſpeak guile: proudly they talk.
9 Againſt the heav'ns they ſet their mouth;
    their tongue through th'earth doth walk.
10 There-

(2)

10 Therefore his people unto them
   have hither turned in,
and waters out of a full cup
   wrung out to them have been.
11 And they have fayd, how can it be
   that God this thing fhould know,
& is there in the higheft one
   knowledge hereof alfo?
12 Loe, thefe are the ungodly ones
   who have tranquillity:
within the world they doe increafe
   in rich ability.
13 Surely in vaine in purity
   cleanfed my heart have I.
14 And hands in innocence have wafht,
   for plagu'd am I dayly:
And every morning chaftered.
15 If I think thus to fay,
   thy childrens generation
   loe then I fhould be ray;
16 And when this poynt to underftand
   cafting I did devife,
the matter too laborious
   appeared in mine eyes.
17 Vntill unto the fanctuary
   of God I went, & then
J prudently did underftand
   the laft end of thefe men.
(*)
18 Surely in places flippery

thefe

these men thou placed hast:
and into desolations
   thou dost them downward cast.

19 As in a moment, how are they
   brought to destruction?
how are they utterly consum'd
   with sad confusion?

20 Like to a dreame when as a man
   awaking doth arise,
so thou o God, when thou awakst
   their Image shalt despise.

21 My heart thus was leaven'd with grief,
   prickt were my reins by mee:

22 So foolish was I, & knew not,
   like a beast before thee.

(4)

23 Neverthelesse continually
   before thee I doe stand:
thou hast upheld mee stedfastly
   also by my right hand.

24 Thou with thy prudent counsell shalt
   guidance unto mee give:
up afterward also thou shalt
   to glory mee receive.

25 In heavn above but thee alone
   who is it that I have?
and there is nothing upon earth
   besides thee that I crave.

25 This flesh of mine, my heart also
   doth faile me altogether:
but God the strength is of my heart,

and

and portion mine for ever.

27 For loe, they that are far from thee
   utterly perish shall:
those who a whoring goe from thee
   thou hast destroyed all.

23 But as for mee, for mee it's good
   neere God for to repaire:
in God the Lord I put my trust,
   all thy works to declare.

Psalme 74
Maschil of Asaph.

O GOD, why hast thou cast us off,
   why doth thy rage indure?
for ever smoaking out against
   the sheep of thy pasture?

2 Thy congregation call to minde
   of old by thee purchast:
the rod of thine inheritance
   which thou redeemed hast,
This mount Sion wherin thou dwelst.

3   Lift up thy foot on hye,
unto the desolations
   of perpetuity:
Thy foe within the Sanctuary
   hath done all lewd designes.

4 Amidst thy Church thy foes doe roare:
   their Banners set for signes.

5 The man that axes on thick trees
   did lift up had renowne:

6 But now with axe & maules at once,
   her carv'd works they beat downe.

7 Thy

PSALM lxxiv.

7 Thy sanctuaryes into fire
  they cast, the dwelling place
 of thy name downe unto the ground
  prophanely they did raze.
8 Let us together them destroy,
  thus in their hearts they sayd:
 Gods Synagogues throughout the land
  all in the flames they layd.

(2)

9 Our signes we see not, there's no more
  a Prophet us among:
 nor with us any to be found
  that understands how long.
10 How long shall the oppressing foe
  o mighty God, defame?
 thine enemy for evermore
  shall he blaspheme thy name?
11 Why dost thou thus withdraw thine hand,
  the right hand of thy strength?
 out of thy bosom o doe thou
  draw it forth to the length.
12 Because the mighty God hath been
  from ancient time my King,
 in middest of the earth he is
  salvation working.
13 Thou diddest by thy mighty powre
  devide the sea asunder:
 the Dragons heads in peeces thou
  didst break the waters under.
14 The heads of the Leviathan
  thou into peeces brake:

to

to people that in defarts dwell
    for meat thou didft him make.
15 Thou clav'ft the fountain & the floud,
    thou dri'dft up flouds of might.
16 Thine is the day, & night is thine:
    thou Sun prepar'ft, & light.
17 Thou all the borders of the earth
    haft conftituted faft :
the fummer & the winter cold
    the fame thou formed haft·
        (1)
18 Remember this, the enemy
    reproachfully doth blame,
o Lord, alfo the foolifh folk
    blafphemed have thy name.
19 O dce not to the multitude
    thy turtles foule deliver:
the congregation of thy poore
    forget not thou for ever.
20 Vnto thy cov'nant have refpect:
    becaufe the dark places
of th'earth with habitations
    are full of furioufnes.
21 O let not the oppreffed one
    returne away with fhame:
o let the poor & needy one
    give prayfe unto thy name.
22 Arife o God, plead thine owne caufe:
    have thou in memorie
how day by day the foolifh man
    with fcorne reproacheth thee.
        S   23 Thine

23 Thine enemyes voyce forget not thou:
  the loud tumult of thofe
continually on high afcends
  that rife thee to oppofe.

Pfalme 75

To the chief mufician Altafchith, pfalme
or fong of Afaph.

O GOD, to thee doe we give thanks,
  thanks give we unto thee:
& that thy name is neere at hand,
  thy wonders fhew to bee.

2 When I th'affembly fhall receive
  uprightly judge I will.

2 Th'earth & its dwellers all do melt:
  I ftay its pillars ftill,

4 I did unto the foolifh fay,
  deale not fo foolifhly:
alfo unto the wicked ones,
  lift not the horne on hye.

5 Lift yee not up your horne on high:
  with ftiffned neck fpeak not,

6 For neither from Eaft, Weft, nor South,
  promotion can be got.

7 But God is judge: he fets up one,
  another downe doth tread.

8 For in the Lords hand is a cup,
  alfo the wine is red:
It's full of mixture, & thereout
  he poures: but on earth all
the wicked ones the dregs therof
  both ftrein, & drink them fhall.

9 But as for me I will declare,   for

for evermore I will
sing prayses unto him that is
    the God of Iacob *still.*
10 Of men ungodly all the hornes
    also cut off will I:
but the hornes of the righteous,
    shall be exalted high.

Psalme 76

To the chief musician, on Neginoth, a psalm
        or song of Asaph

IN Iudah God is knowne: his name
    is great in Israell.
2 In Salem also is his tent:
    in Sion he doth dwell,
3 There brake he th'arrows of the bow,
    the shield, sword, & battell.   Selah.
4 Illustrious thou art, thou dost
    the mounts of prey excell.
5 They that are stout of heart are spoyld,
    they slept their sleep profound:
and of the men of might there is
    none that their hands have found.
6 Of Iacob o thou mighty God,
    as thy rebuke our past,
the chariot also, & the horse
    in a dead sleepe are cast.
            (2)
7 Thou ev'n thou art to be feared,
    and who is it before
thy presence that can stand, when as
    that thou art angry sore?
8 Thou diddest cause for to be heard   judge.

judgement from heav'n above:
the earth exceedingly did feare,
also it did not move.
9 When as the mighty God arose,
to th' execution
of judgement, to save all the meek
that are the earth upon.   Selah.
10 Assuredly unto thy prayse,
shall turne the wrath of man:
& the remainder of the earth
also thou shalt restraine.
11 Vow, & pay to the Lord your God;
that him surround ail yee,
and bring ye presents unto him,
that feared ought to bee.
12 The spirit that in Princes is,
asunder cut he shall:
unto the Kings on earth that be,
dreadfull he is *withall*.
Psalme 77
To the chief musician, to Ieduthun, a
psalme of Asaph.
TO GOD I cryed with my voyce:
yea with my voyce I have
cryed unto the mighty God;
and eare to mee he gave.
2 In my distresse I sought the Lord:
my sore ran in the night,
& ceased not: also my soule
refused comfort quite.
3 I did remember God, also

disqui.

disquieted was I:
I did complaine, & my spirit
o'rewhelmd was heavily.   Selah.

4 Awaking thou dost hold mine eyes:
I cannot speak for feares.

5 I have considered dayes of old,
of ancient times the yeares.

(2)

6 To my remembrance I doe call
the song in night I had:
I commun'd with my heart, also
strict search my spirit made.

7 For ever will the Lord cast off?
& pleasd will he not bee?

8 His tender mercy is it ceast
to perpetuitee?
His promise doth it, faile for aye?

9 Hath God forgot likewise
gracious to be? hath he shut up
in wrath his deare mercyes?   Selah.

10 Then did I say, within my selfe,
tis mine infirmity:
the yeares of the right hand I will
think on of the most high.

(3)

11 I will unto remembrance call
the actions of the Lord:
thy wondrous works of ancient time
surely I will record.

12 I'le muse also of all thy works,
& of thy doings talk.

S 3   13 with-

13 Within the temple is thy way,
   o God, *where thou dost walk.*
  What god so great as our God is?
   1 *W*orks wonderfull that are
  thou God hast done; among the folk
   thou dost thy strength declare.
15 Those that thy people are thou hast
   with thine owne arme set free,
 of Iacob also of Ioseph
   the childeren that bee.   Selah.
      (4)
16 Thee did the waters see, o God,
   thee did the waters see:
 they were afraid, the deeps also
   could not but troubled bee.
17 With waters were the clouds pour'd forth,
   the skies a sound out sent:
 also thine arrows on each side
   abroad dispersed went.
18 Thy thunders voyce in heaven was:
   the world illuminate
 thy lightnings did, the earth also
   trembled & shook hereat.
19 Thy wayes ith sea, thy paths & steps
   unkowne, are in the deep.
20 By Moses & by Arons hand
   thou ledst thy folk like sheep.
    Psalme 78
    Maschil of Asaph.
GIve listning eare unto my law,
  yee people that are mine,

                unto

unto the sayings of my mouth
   doe yee your eare incline.
2 My mouth I'le ope in parables,
   I'le speak hid things of old:
3 Which we have heard & knowne:& which
   our fathers have us told.
4 Them from their children wee'l not hide,
   to th'after age shewing
  the Lords prayses: his strength, & works
   of his wondrous doing.
5 In Iacob he a witnesse set,
   & put in Ifraell
  a law, which he our fathers charg'd,
   they should their children tell:
6 That th'age to come & children which
   are to be borne might know;
  that they might rise up & the same
   unto their children show.
7 That they upon the mighty God
   their confidence might set:
  and Gods works & his commandment
   might keep & not forget,
8 And might not like their fathers be,
   a stiffe, stout race; a race
  that set not right their hearts: nor firme
   with God their spirit was.
(2)
9 The armed sonnes of Ephraim,
   that went out with their bowe,
  did turne their backs in the day when
   they did to battell goe.

10 Gods

10 Gods cov'nant they kept not: to walk
     in his law they denyde:

11 His works, & wonders, they forgot,
     that he to them descryde.

12 Things that were mervielous he did
     within their fathers sight:
  in Egipts land, within the field
     of Zoan, *by his might*.

13 He did devide the sea, also
     he caus'd them through to passe:
  & he the waters made to stand
     that as an heap it was.

14 With cloud by day, with fire all night

15   he led them; Rocks he clave
  in wildernes, as from great deeps
     drink unto them he gave.

16 Ev'n from out of the stony rock
     streames he did bring also,
  & caused water to run downe
     like as the rivers do.

(3)

17 Moreover they did adde yet more
     against him for to sin:
  by their provoaking the most high
     the wildernes within.

18 And also they within their heart
     did tempt the God of might:
  by asking earnestly for meat
     for their soules appetite:

19 Moreover they against God spake:
     they sayd can God be able

within

within the defart wildernes
  to furnifh us a table:
20 Loe, he the rock fmote, thence gufht out
  waters, & ftreames did flow:
for his folk can he flefh provide,
  can he give bread alfo?
21 The Lord heard, he was wroth for this,
  fo kindled was a fire
'gainft Iacob:&'gainft Ifraell
  there came up wrathfull ire.
22 For they in God believed not:
  nor in his health did hope:
23 Though from above he charg'd the clouds:
  & doores of heav'n fet ope:
                (4)
24 Manna to eate he raind on them;
  & gave them the heavns wheat.
25 Each man of them ate Angells food:
  to th'full he fent them meate.
26 Ith heav'ns he made the Eaft-winde blow:
  brought South-winde by his powre.
27 He flefh on them like duft: wing'd foules
  like the feas fand did fhowre.
28 And in the middeft of their camp
  he caufed it to fall,
ev'n round about on every fide
  their dwelling places all.
29 So they did eate, they filled were
  abundantly alfo:
for that which was their owne defire
  he did on them beftow:
          T   30 How-

30 Howbeit they were not eſtrang'd
    from their luſtfull deſire:
  but while their meat was in their mouths,
31   Vpon them came Gods ire,
    And ſlew their fat ones: & ſmote downe
    of Iſraell the choiſe men.
32 Still for all this they ſin'd: nor did
    believe his wonders then.

(5)

33 Therefore he did in vanity
    the dayes of their life ſpend,
  and haſtily he brought their yeares
    vnto a fearfull *end*.
34 When he them ſlew, then after him
    they ſought with their deſire:
  and they return'd, early alſo
    did after God enquire.
35 Likewiſe that God was their ſtrong rock
    they cal'd to memoree:
  and that the mighty God moſt high,
    was their Redeemer free.
36 Yet with their mouth they flattred him
    and to him their tongues lyde.
37 For right their heart was not in them:
    nor did in's cov'nant byde.
38 But full of mercy, he forgave
    their ſin, & ſtroyd them not;
  yea, oft he turn'd his wrath aſide,
    nor rayſ'd all's anger hot.
39 For he, that they were but fraile fleſh,
    and as it were a winde

                                    that

PSALME lxxviii.

that passeth, & comes not againe,
  recalled unto minde.

(6)

40 How oft in desart vext they him:
  and made him there to moane?
41 Yea, they turn'd, tempted God: & did
  stint Isr'ells holy one.
42 His hand they did not, nor the day
  keep in their remembrance:
wherein he from the enemy
  gave them deliverance:
43 And how his signes miraculous
  in Egipt he had showne:
and his most fearfull prodigies
  within the field of Zoan:
44 Also how he their rivers had
  converted into bloud:
& (that they could not drink therof)
  the waters of their floud.
45 Amongst them, which did them devoure,
  he sent forth divers flies:
& them amongst, which them destroyd,
  he sent forth frogs likewise.
46 He gave their fruit to th'Caterpillar:
  their labour to th'Locust.
47 He did their Vines destroy with haile:
  their Sycamores with frost.
48 Also unto the haile he did
  their cattell shut up fast:
likewise their heards of cattell to
  the fiery thunder blast,

T 2   49 He

49 He caſt on them fierce ire, & wrath,
   & indignation,
  & ſore diſtreſſe: by ſending forth
   ill Angells them upon.

(7)

50 He made a way unto his wrath,
   and their ſoule did not ſave
from death: alſo their life over
   to Peſtilence he gave,
51 He within Egipt land alſo
   all the firſt borne did ſmite:
thoſe that within the tents of Ham
   were chiefeſt of their might:
52 But he made like a flock of ſheep
   his owne folk forth to go:
like to a flock ith wildernes
   he guided them alſo.
53 And he in ſafety did them lead
   ſo that they did not dread:
within the ſea their enemies
   he alſo covered.
54 And to the border he did bring
   them of his holy place:
unto this mountaine which he did
   by his right hand purchaſe.
55 Fore them he caſt the heathen our,
   their lot he did devide
by line: & Iſr'ells tribes he made
   in their tents to abide.

(8)

56 Yet they tempted the moſt high God,

                  and

& griev'd him bitterly:
also his testimonyes they
kept not *attentively*:
57 But like their fathers back they turn'd
and faithlesnesse did show:
they turned were aside ev'n like
to a deceitfull bowe.
58 For they to anger did provoake
him with their places hye:
& with their graven Images,
mov'd him to jealousy.
59 God hearing this, was wroth, & loath'd
Isr'ell with hatred great:
60 So Shiloh s tent he left: the tent
which men amongst he set,
61 And he delivered his strength
into captivity:
also into the enemies hand
his beautifull glory.
62 To th' sword he gave his folk: & was
wroth with his heritage.
63 Fire their young men devour'd:their maides
none gave to marriage.
64 Their Priests fell by the sword: also
their widdows did not weepe.
65 Then did the Lord arise as one
awakned out of sleepe:
Like a strong man that after wine
65 doth shout. He also smote
his foes behinde: & so he gave
them an eternall blot.

T 3   67 Then

67 Then he did Iosephs tent refuse:
    nor Ephr'ims tribe approv'd.
68 But he the tribe of Iudah chose:
    mount Sion which he lov'd.
69 And he his Sanctuary built
    like unto places high:
    like to the earth which he did found
    to perpetuity.
70 Of David also his servant
    election he did make,
    and from the place of folding up
    the sheep he did him take.
71 From following the ewes with young
    he did him then advance;
    to feed Iacob his folk, also
    Isr'ell his heritance.
72 So he according to his hearts
    integrity them fed:
    and by the wise discretion
    of his hands he them led.

Psalme 79
A psalme of Asaph.

O GOD, the heathen entred have
   thine heritance, & defylde
thine holy temple: they on heaps
    Ierusalem have pylde.
2 The dead bodyes of thy servants
   they given have for meate
to th' fowles of heav'n: flesh of thy Saints
    for beasts of earth to eate.

PSALME lxxix.

3 Their bloud they have forth powred round
about Ierufalem
like unto waters: & there *was*
none for to bury *them.*

4 To thofe that neere unto us dwell
reproach become are wee:
a fcoffing & a fcorne to them
that round about us bee.

5 How long, Iehovah, wilt thou ftill
continue in thine ire,
for ever? fhall thy jealoufie
burne like as doth the fire?

6 Vpon the heathen poure thy wrath
which never did thee know,
upon the kingdomes that have not
cal'd on thy name alfo.

7 Becaufe they Iacob have devour'd:
his habitation
they alfo wondroufly have brought
to defolation.

(2)

8 Minde not againft us former fins,
let thy mercies make haft
us to prevent: becaufe we are
neere utterly layd wafte.

9 God of our fafety, help thou us
for thy names glory make,
us free alfo, & purge away
our fin for thy names fake.

10 Why fay the heathen where's their God?
with heathen let be knowne

before

before our eyes, the vengeance of
   thy servants bloud out flowne.
11 Before thee let the prisoners sighs
   come up, accordingly
as is thy mighty arme: save those
   that are design'd to dye,
12 And to our neighbours seven fold,
   into their bosome pay,
that their reproach, with which o Lord,
   reproached thee have they.
13 So we thy folk & pasture sheepe,
   will give thee thanks alwayes:
and unto generations all,
   wee will shew forth thy prayse.

Psalme 80

To the chief musician upon Shoshannim
   Eduth, a psalme of Asaph.

O Isr'ells shepheard, give thou eare;
   that Ioseph leadst about
like as a flock: that dwelst betweene
   the Cherubims, shine out.
2 Before Ephr'im & Benjamin,
   Manasseh s tribe also,
doe thou stir up thy strength, & come,
   and to us safety show.
3 O God returne thou us againe,
   and cause thy countenance
to shine forth upon us; so wee
   shall have deliverance.
4 Lord God of hoasts, how long wilt thou
   be wroth at thy folks prayrs?

thou

5 Thou feedst with bread of tears, & them
    to drink giv'st many teares.
6 A strife unto our neighbours us
    thou dost also expose:
and scornefully amongst themselves
    laugh at us doe our foes.
7 O God of hoasts, turne us againe,
    & cause thy countenance
to shine forth upon us, so wee
    shall have deliverance.

(2)

8 Thou hast brought out of Egipt land
    a Vine, thou diddest cast
the heathen people forth, also
    this *vine* thou planted hast.
9 Before it thou prepared hast
    a roome where it might stand:
deep root thou didst cause it to take
    and it did fill the land.
10 Her shade hid hills, & her boughs did
    like Cedars great *extend.*
11 Her boughs to th'sea, & her branches
    she to the floud did send.
12 Why hast thou then her hedges made
    quite broken downe to lye,
so that all those doe pluck at her
    that in the way passe by?
13 The Boare from out the wood he doth
    by wasting it annoy:
& wilde beasts of the field doe it
    devouringly destroy.

V

(3)

14 Wee doe befeech thee to returne
o God of hoafts, incline
to look from heaven, & behould,
& vifit thou this vine.

15 The vineyard which thou haft alfo
with thy right hand fet faft,
that branch likewife which for thy felfe
ftrongly confirm'd thou haft.

16 It is confumed with the fire
and utterly cut downe,
perifh they doe, & that becaufe
thy countenance doth frowne.

17 Vpon the man of thy right hand
let thine hand prefent bee:
upon the fon of man whom thou
haft made fo ftrong for thee

18 So then from henceforth wee will not
from thee goe back at all:
o doe thou quicken us, & wee
upon thy name will call.

19 Lord God of hoafts, turne us againe,
and caufe thy countenance
to fhine forth upon us, fo wee
fhall have deliverance.

Pfalme 81
To the chiefe mufician upon Gittith,
a pfalme of Afaph.

SIng unto God who is our ftrength,
and that with a loud voyce:
unto him that is Iacobs God

make

make yee a joyfull noyſe.

2 Take up a pſalme of melodie,
    and bring the Timbrel hither:
the Harp *which ſoundes* ſo pleaſantly
    with Pſaltery together.

3 As in the time of the new moone
    with Trumpet ſound on high:
in the appoynted time & day
    of our ſolemnity.

4 Becauſe that unto Iſraell
    this thing a ſtatute was;
and by the God of Iacob this
    did for a judgement paſs.

5 This witneſſe he in Ioſeph ſet
    when as through Egipt land
he went: I there a language heard
    I did not underſtand.

6 I from the burden which he bare
    his ſhoulder did ſet ſree:
his hands alſo were from the pots
    delivered by mee.

(2)

7 Thou cal'dſt in ſtreights, & I thee freed:
    in thunders ſecret way
I anſwred thee, I prov'd thee at
    waters of Meribah.   Selah.

8 Heare o my people, & I will
    teſtifie unto thee:
o Iſraell, if that thou wilt
    attention give to mee.

9 Any ſtrange god there ſhall not be

in midſt of thee at all:
nor unto any forrein god
 thou bowing downe ſhalt fall.
10 I am the Lord thy God who thee
from land of Egipt led:
 thy mouth ope wide, & thou by mee
 with plenty ſhalt be fed.
11 My people yet would not give eare
 unto the voyce I ſpake:
and Iſraell would not in mee
 quiet contentment take.
12 So in the hardnes of their heart
 I did them ſend away,
in their owne conſultations
 likewiſe *then* walked they.

(3)

13 O that my people unto mee
 obedient had bin:
and o that Iſraell he had
 walked my wayes within.
14 I ſhould within a little time
 have pulled downe their foes:
I ſhould have turn'd my hand upon
 ſuch as did them oppoſe.
15 The haters of the Lord to him
 obedience ſhould have faynd:
but unto perpetuity
 their time ſhould have remaind.
16 And with the fineſt of the wheat
 have nouriſht them ſhould hee:
with honie of the rock I ſhould

have

PSALME lxxxii.

have satiffied thee.

Pſalme 82
A pſalme of Aſaph.

THe mighty God doth ſtand within
  th'aſſemblie of the ſtrong:
and he it is that righteouſly
  doth judge the gods among.

2 How long a time is it that yee
  will judge unrighteouſlie?
& will accept the countenance
  of thoſe that wicked bee?

3 See that yee doe defend the poore,
  alſo the fatherleſſe:
unto the needy juſtice doe,
  and that are in diſtreſſe.

4 The waſted poore, & thoſe that are
  needy deliver yee;
and them redeeme out of the hand
  of ſuch as wicked bee.

5 They know not, nor will underſtand,
  in darknes they walk on:
all the foundations of the earth
  quite out of courſe are gone.

6 I ſayd that yee are gods, & ſonnes
  of th'higheſt yee are all.

7 But yee ſhall dye like men, & like
  one of the princes fall.

8 That thou mayſt judge the earth o God,
  doe thou thy ſelfe advance;
for thou ſhalt have the nations
  for thine inheritance.

V 3   PSALM

Pſalme 8 3

A pſalme or ſong of Aſaph,

O GOD, doe not thou ſilence keep:
  o doe not thou refraine
thy ſelfe from ſpeaking, & o God.
  doe not thou dumb remaine.

2 For loe, thine enemies that be
  doe rage tumultuouſly:
& they that haters be of thee
  have lift the head on hye.

3 Againſt thoſe that thy people be
  they crafty counſell take;
alſo againſt thy hidden ones
  they conſultation make.

4 They ſayd, left they a nation be,
  let's cut them downe therefore,
that in remembrance Iſr'elſs name
  may not be any more.

5 For they together taken have
  counſell with one conſent,
and in confederation
  againſt thee they are bent.

6 The tabernacles of Edom
  and of the Iſhmaelites:
the people of the Haggarens
  & of the Moabites.

7 The men of Gebal, with Ammon,
  and Amaleck conſpire,
the Philiſtims, with them that be
  inhabitants of Tyre.

8 Aſſyria morover is

con-

conjoyned unto them:
& help they have adminiſtred
unto Lots childerren.

(2)

9 **As** thou didſt to the Middianites,
ſo to them be it dore:
as unto Siſera & Iabin
at the Brook of Kiſon

10 Who neere to Endor ſuddenly
were quite diſcomfited:
who alſo did become as dung
that on the earth is *ſprea*.

11 Like unto Oreb, & like Zeeb
make thou their Nobles fall,
yea, as Zeba & Zalmunna
make thou their Princes all.

12 Who ſayd, for our poſſeſſion
Gods houſes let us take.

13 My God, thou like a wheel, like ſtraw
before the winde them make.

14 **As** fire doth burne a wood, & as
the flame ſets hills on fire:

15 So with thy tempeſt them purſue,
& fright them in thine ire.

16 Doe thou their faces all fill full
of ignominious ſhame:
that ſo they may o Lord, be made
to ſeek after thy name.

17 Confounded let them ever be,
and terriblie troubled:
yea, let them be put unto ſhame,

and bee extinguished.

28 That men may know; that thou whose name
    IEHOVAH is only,
art over all the earth throughout
advanced the most high.

Psalme 84

To the chief musician upon Gittith a psalm
for the sonnes of Korah.

HOw amiable Lord of hoasts
    thy tabernacles bee?
2 My soule longs for Iehovahs courts,
    yea it ev'n faints in mee.
Mine heart, my flesh also cryes out
    after the living God:
3 Yea ev'n the sparrow hath found out
    an house *for hir aboad.*
Also the swallow *findes* her nest
    thine Altars *neere unto*
where shee her young layes: Lord of hoasts,
    my King, my God also.
4 Blest they that dwell within thy house:
    still they will give thee prayse.   Selah.
5 Blest is the man whose strength's in thee,
    in whose heart are their wayes.
6 Who as they passe through Baca's Vale
    doe make it a fountaine:
also the pooles *that are therin*
    are filled full of raine:
7 From strength to strength they go: to God
    in Sion all appeare.
8 Lord God of hoasts, o heare my pra'yr,
                  o Iacobs

o Iacobs God, give eare.   Selah.

(2)

9 Behould o God our shield: the face
    of thine annoynted see.

10 For better's in thy courts a day,
      then *elsewhere* thousands bee:
    I rather had a doore-keeper
      be it'h house of my God:
    then in the tents of wickednes
      to settle mine aboad.

11 Because the Lord God is a Sun,
      he is a shield also:
    Iehovah *on his people* grace
      and glory will bestow:
    No good thing will he hould from them
      that doe walk uprightlee.

12 O Lord of hoasts, the man is blest
      that put his trust in thee.

Psalme 85

To the chiefe musician, a psalme for the
      sonnes of Korah.

O LORD, thou hast been to the land
    gracious: Iacobs captiuity
  thou hast returned *with thy hand.*

2 Thou *also* the iniquity
      of thy people hast pardoned:
    thou all their sin hast covered.   Selah.

3 Thou all thine anger didst withdraw:
      from thy fierce indignation
    thou hast thy selfe turned away.

4 O God of our salvation

                    W   convert

convert thou us; & doe thou make
thine anger toward us to flake.

5 Shall thy wrath ever be us on?
wilt thou thine indignation
draw out to generation?
and unto generation?

6   Wilt thou not us reviv'd let bee
that thy folk may rejoyce in thee.

(2)

7 Lord on us shew thy mercy; eke
thy saving health on us bestow.

8 I'le hark what God the Lord will speak,
for hee'l speak peace his folk unto,
and to his Saints: but let not them
to foolishnes returne agen.

9 Surelyhis saving health is nigh
unto all them that doe him feare;
that in our land may dwell glory.

10 Mercy & truth met *together*,
prosperiry & righteousnes
embracing did *each other* kiss.

11   Truth springs out of the earth: also
from heaven looketh righteousnes.

12 Yea, God shall that that's good bestow
our land eke shall give her increase.

13 Iustice shall goe before his face,
& in the way her steps shall place.

Another of the same

O LORD, thou favour'd haft thy land:
  Iacobs captivity.

2 Thou haft brought back: thou pard'ned haft

thy

thy folks iniquity:
Thou haſt cloſe coverd all their ſin.

3   Thy wrath away all caſt
thou haſt: from fiercenes of thine ire
thy ſelfe return'd thou haſt.

4   Convert us back, o thou the God
of our ſalvation:
& toward us cauſe thou to ceaſe
thine indignation,

5   Wilt thou be angry ſtill with us
for evermore? what ſhall?
thine anger be by thee drawne-out
to generations all?

6   Wilt thou not us revive? in thee
thy folk rejoyce ſhall ſo.

7   Shew us thy mercy, Lord; on us
thy ſaving health beſtow.

(2)

8   I'le heare what God the Lord will ſpeak:
for to his people peace
hee'l ſpeak, & to his Saints: leſt they
returne to fooliſhnes.

9   Surely naere them that doe him feare
is his ſalvation:
that glory may within our land
have habitation.

10   Mercy & truth doe joyntly meet:
juſtice & peace doe kiſſe.

11   Truth ſprings from earth: & rightouſnes
from heaven looking is.

12   Yea what is good the Lord ſhall give:

and yeild her fruit our land.
13 Iuſtice ſhall 'fore him goe: & make
her ſteps i'th way to ſtand.

Pſalme 86
A prayer of David.

Bow downe o Lord, thine eare,
& harken unto mee:
becauſe that I afflicted am,
alſo I am needie.

2 Doe thou preſerve my ſoule,
for gracious am I:
o thou my God, thy ſervant ſave,
that doth on thee rely.

3 Lord pitty me, for I
daily cry thee unto.

4 Rejoyce thy ſervants ſoule: for Lord,
to thee mine lift I do.

5 For thou o Lord, art good,
to pardon prone withall:
and to them all in mercy rich
that doe upon thee call.

6 Iehovah, o doe thou
give eare my pray'r unto:
& of my ſupplications
attend the voyce alſo.

7 In day of my diſtreſſe,
to thee I will complaine:
by reaſon that thou unto mee
wilt anſwer give againe.

(2)

8 Amongſt the gods, o Lord,

none is there like to thee:
neither with thine are any work
that may compared bee.

9   All nations o Lord,
whom thou haſt made, *the ſame*
ſhall come & worſhip thee before:
and glorify thy Name.

10   Becauſe thou mighty art,
the things that thou haſt done
are wonderfull, thou art thy ſelfe
the mighty God alone.

11   Iehovah, unto mee
o make thy way appeare,
walk in thy truth I will; mine heart
unite thy name to feare.

12   Withall mine heart I will
o Lord my God, thee prayſe:
& I will glorify thy name,
for evermore *alwayes.*

13   Becauſe that unto mee
thy mercy doth excell;
alſo thou haſt delivered
my ſoule from loweſt hell.

(3)

14   O God, the proud, & troups
of violent roſe 'gainſt mee,
after my ſoule they ſought: nor have
before them placed thee.

15   But Lord thou art a God,
tender, & gracious;
longſuffring, & in mercy thou

W 2   and

& truth art plenteous.

16   O turne thou unto mee,
      and mercy on mee have:
   unto thy servant give thy strength:
      thine handmaides son do save.

17   Mee shew a signe for good,
      that mine haters may see,
  and be asham'd; because Lord, thou
      dost help, & comfort mee.

Psalme 87

A psalme or song for the sonnes
of Korah.

Among the holy hills
   is his foundation.

2 More then all Iacobs tents, the Lord
    loves the gates of Sion.

3   Things glorious spoken are
     o Gods citty, of thee.   Selah.

4 I'le mention Rahab, & Babel,
    to them that doe know mee;
    Behold Philistia,
    Tyrus *citty* likewise,
  with Ethiopia; that this man
    by birth did thence arise.

5   Also it shall be sayd,
     of Sion that borne there
  this & that man was, & the high'st
    himselfe shall stablish her.

6   Iehovah he shall co unt,
    ev'n at that time when as,
  the people he doth number up,

that

that there this man borne was.　　Selah

7　Both thofe that fingers are
　as alfo *there fhall bee,*
thofe that on inftruments doe play:
　all my fprings are in thee.

Pfalme 88

A fong or pfalme for the fons of Korah, to
the chief mufician up̄o Mahalath Leannoth,
Mafchil of Heman the
Ezrahite.

LORD God of my falvation,
　before thee day & night cryde I.
2　Before thee o let my pray'r come:
　incline thine eare unto my cry.
3　Becaufe my foule is troubled fo:
　and my life draws nigh to the grave.
4　Counted with them to'th pit that go:
　I'me as a man that no ftrength have.
5　Free among thofe men that be dead,
　like flaine which in the grave are fhut;
　by thee noe more remembered:
　and by thy hand off are they cut.
6　Thou haft mee layd i'th pit moft low
　in dakrneffes, within deep caves.
7　Hard on mee lyes thy wrath, & thou
　doft mee afflict with all thy waves.　　Selah.
8　Men that of mine acquaintance bee
　thou haft put far away mee fro:
　unto them loathfome thou madft mee,
　I am fhut up nor forth can go.
9　Becaufe of mine affliction,

　　　　　　　　　　　　　mine

mine eye with mourning pines away:
Iehovah, I call thee upon:
& stretch my hands to thee all day;

(2)

10 Shew wonders to the dead wilt thou?
shall dead arise & thee confess? Selah.

11 I'th grave wilt thou thy kindenes show?
in lost estate thy faithfullues?

12 Thy works that wonderfull have been
within the dark shal they be knowne?
& shall thy righteousnes *be seene*
in the land of oblivion?

13 But Lord I have cryde thee unto
at morne, my pray'r prevent shall thee.

14 Lord why casts thou my soule thee fro?
why hidest thou thy face from mee?

15 I'me poore afflicted, & to dye
am ready, from my youthfull yeares,
I am sore troubled doubtfully
while I doe beare thy horrid feares.

16 Thy fierce wrath over mee doth goe,
thy terrors they doe mee dismay.

17 Encompasse mee about they doe,
close mee together all the day.

18 Lover & friend a far thou hast
removed off away from mee,
& mine acquaintance thou hast cast
into darksom obscuritee.

Psalme 89
Maschil of Ethan the
Ezrahite.

PSALM

THe mercyes of Iehovah sing
   for evermore will I:
I 'le with my mouth thy truth make known
   to all posterity.
2 For I have sayd that mercy shall
   for ever be up built;
establish in the very heav'ns
   thy faithfullnes thou wilt.
3 With him that is my chosen one
   I made a covenant:
& by *an oath* have sworne unto
   David mine owne servant.
4 To perpetuity thy seed
   establish-sure I will:
also to generations all
   thy throne I 'le build up *still*.   Selah.
5 Also the heav'ns thy wonders Lord,
   they shall with prayse confess;
in the assemblie of the Saints
   also thy faithfullnes.
6 For who can be compar'd unto
   the Lord the heav'ns within?
'mong sonnes of mighty to the Lord
   who is't that's like to him.

(2)

7 I'th Saints assemblie greatly God
   is to be had in feare:
and to be reverenc't of all those
   that round about him are.
8 Lord God of hoasts, what Lord like thee
   in power doth abide?

thy faithfullnes doth compasse thee
 also on every side.
9 Over the raging of the sea,
   thou dost dominion beare:
 when as the waves therof arise,
   by thee they stilled are.
10 Like to one slaine, thou broken hast
   in pieces Rahab quite:
 thou hast disperst thine enemies
   ev'n by thine arme of might.
11 The heav'ns together with the earth,
   thine are they: thine they bee;
 the world, with fullnes of the same,
   founded they were by thee.
12 The North together with the South
   thou didst create the same:
 Tabor together with Hermon,
   rejoyce shall in thy Name.
(3)
13 Thou hast a very mighty arme,
   thy hand it is mighty,
 and also thy right hand it is
   exalted up on high.
14 Iustice & judgement of thy throne
   are the prepared place:
 mercy & truth preventing shall
   goe forth before thy face.
15 O blessed are the people that
   the joyfull sound doe know,
 Lord, in thy countenances light
   they up & downe shall goe:

16 They

16 They shall in thy name all the day
    rejoyce exceedingly:
and in thy righteousnes they shall
    be lifted up on high.

17 Becaufe that thou art unto them
    the glory of their powre:
our horne shall be exalted high,
    alfo in thy favour.

18 Becaufe Iehovah is to us
    a fafe protection;
and he that is our Soveraigne,
    is Ifr'ells Holy-one.

(4)

19 Then didft thou fpeake in vifion,
    unto thy Saint, & fayd,
I upon one that mighty is
    falvation have layd:
One from the folk chofe, I fet up.

20 David my fervant I
have found: him I annoynted with
    mine oyle of fanctity.

21 With whom my hand shall ftablisht be;
    mine arme him ftrengthen shall.

22 Alfo the enemy shall not
    exact on him at all:
Nor shall the Son of wickednes
    afflict him any more.

23 Before him I'le beat downe his focs,
    and plague his haters fore.

24 My mercy, truth, shall be with him;
    & in my name shall be

his

25 his horne exalted. And I'le set
    his hand upon the sea:
I'th rivers alſo his right hand.
26   He ſhall cry mee unto,
  thou art my Father: & my God,
    Rock of my health alſo.
27 Alſo I will make him to be
    my firſt begotten one:
higher then thoſe that Princes are,
    who dwell the earth upon.
28 My mercy I will keep for him
    to times which ever laſt:
alſo my covenant with him
    it ſhall ſtand very faſt.
(5)
29 And I will make his ſeed indure
    to perpetuitee:
his throne likewiſe it like unto
    the dayes of heav'n ſhall bee.
30 If that his ſons forſake my law,
    & from my judgements ſwerve:
31 If they my ſtattutes break, & my
    commandes doe not obſerve:
32 Then will I viſit with the rod
    their bold tranſgreſſion,
as alſo their iniquity
    with ſore ſtripes *them upon*.
33 But yet my loving kindenes, it
    I'le not take utterly
away from him: nor will ſuffer
    my faithfullnes to lye.

34 The covenant I made with him
  by mee shall not be broke:
neither will I alter the thing
  which by my lips is spoke.
35 Once sware I by my holines,
  if I to David lye:
36 His seed asuredly shall last
  to perpetuity:
And like the Sun 'fore mee his throne.
37   It like the moone for aye
shall be establish't, like a true
  witnesse in heav'n: Selah.
(6)
38 But thou hast cast off, & us had
  in detestation:
exceedingly thou hast been wroth
  with thine annoynted one.
39 Thou hast made voyd the covenant
  of thy servant, his crowne
thou hast prophan'd unto the ground
  by casting of it downe.
40 Thou hast broke all his hedges downe:
  his forts thou ruin'd hast.
41 All those doe make a spoyle of him
  who by the way have past:
Hee's a reproach to his neighbours.
42   Of them that him annoy
thou hast advanced their right hand:
  & made all's foes to joy.
43 The sharp edge also of his sword
  thou hast turn'd backward quite:

X 3   and

and in the battell thou haſt not
made him to ſtand upright.

44 Thou haſt made alſo for to ceaſe
his glorious renowne:
unto the very earth his throne
thou alſo haſt caſt downe.

45 And of his youthfull yeares the dayes
thou haſt diminiſhed;
with very great confuſion
thou haſt him covered.   Selah.

(7)

46 How long? Iehovah, wilt thou hide
thy ſelfe for evermore?
burne like unto conſuming fire
ſhall thy diſpleaſure ſore?

47 To thy remembrance doe thou call
how ſhort a time have I;
wherefore haſt thou created all
mens ſonnes to vanity?

48 What ſtrong man is there that doth live,
& death ſhall never ſee?
from the ſtrong power of the grave
ſhall he his ſoule ſet free?

49 Thy former loving kindeneſſes
o Lord, where are they now?
which in thy truth & faithfullnes
to David thou didſt vow.

50 Lord, the reproach of thy ſervants
unto remembrance call:
how I it beare in my boſome
from mighty people all.

51 Wher-

51 Wherewith thy adverſaryes Lord,
    have caſt reproach upon,
  wherewith they have reproacht the ſteps
    of thine annointed one.
52 O let Iehovah be bleſſed
    to all eternitee:
  Amen, *ſo let it be*, alſo
    Amen, *ſo it ſhall bee.*

THE

Fovrth Booke

Pſalme 90.
A prayer of Moſes the man of God.
O LORD, thou haſt been unto us
    from generation,
  to generation, a place
    of fixed manſion.
2 Before the mountaines were brought forth,
    ere earth & world by thee
  were form'd: thou art eternally
    God to eternitee.
3 Thou doſt unto deſtruction
    turne miſerable men:
  and then thou ſayſt yee ſonnes of men
    doe yee returne agen.
4 For why o Lord, a thouſand yeares
    are but within thy ſight
  as yeſterday when it is paſt:

and

and as a watch by night.
5 By thee like as it were a flood
    they quite away are borne,
they like a sleep, & as the grasse
    that grows up in the morne.
6 It in the morning flourisheth,
    it also up doth grow;
it in the ev'ning is cut downe
    it withereth also.
7 Because wee by thine anger are
    consumed speedily:
and by thy sore displeasure wee
    are troubled suddenly.
8 Thou hast set our iniquityes
    before thee in thy sight:
our secret evills are within
    thy countenances light.
9 Because in thine exceeding wrath
    our dayes all passe away:
our years wee have consumed quite,
    ev'n as a tale *are they*.

(2)

10 Threescore & ten yeares are the dayes
    of our yeares which remaine,
& if through strength they fourscore be,
    their strength is grief & paine:
For it's cut off soone, & wee flye
11 away: Who is't doth know
thine angers strength? according as
    thy feare, thy wrath is so.
12 Teach us to count our dayes: our hearts

ſo wee'l on wiſdome ſet.

13 Turne Lord, how long? of thy ſervants
   let it repent thee yet?
14 O give us ſatiſſaction
   betimes with thy mercee:
that ſo rejoyce, & be right glad,
   through all our dayes may wee.
15 According to the dayes *wherin*
   affliction wee have had,
and yeares *wherin* wee have ſeen ill,
   now alſo make us glad.
16 Vnto thoſe that thy ſervants be
   doe thou thy work declare:
alſo thy comely glory to
   thoſe that thy children are.
17 Let our Gods beauty be on us,
   our handy works alſo
ſtabliſh on us; our handy work
   eſtabliſh it doe thou.

Pſalme 91.

HE that within the ſecret place
   of the moſt high doth dwell,
he under the Almightyes ſhade
   ſhall lodge himſelfe *full well.*
2 My hope he is, & my fortreſſe,
   I to the Lord will ſay:
he is my God; & I in him
   my confidence will ſtay.
3 Surely out of the fowlers ſnare
   he ſhall deliver thee,
alſo thee from the Peſtilence

         v   infect-

infectious shall free.

4 He with his feathers hide thee shall,
　under his wings shall bee
thy trust: his truth shall be a shield
　and buckler unto thee.

5 Thou shalt not be dismaide with feare
　for terrour by the night:
nor for the arrow that with speed
　flyeth in the day light:

6 Nor for the Pestilence that doth
　walk in the darknes fast:
nor for the sore destruction
　that doth at noone day wast.

(2)

7 A thousand shall fall at thy side,
　& ten thousand also
at thy right hand, but it shall not
　approach thee neere unto:

8 Only thou with thine eyes this thing
　attentively shalt view:
also thou shalt behold how that
　the wicked have their due.

9 Because Iehovah who hath been
　my safe protection,
ev'n the most high, thou hast him made
　thine habitation.

10 Not any thing that evill is
　there shall to thee befall,
neither shall any plague come nigh
　thy dwelling place at all.

11 Because that he his Angells will

　　　　　　　　　comand

command concerning thee:
in all thy wayes *where thou doſt* walk
   thy keeper for to bee.
12 They ſhall ſupport thee in their hands:
   leſt thou againſt a ſtone
13 ſhouldſt daſh thy foot. Thou trample ſhalt
   on thʻAdder, & Lion:
The Lion young & Dragon thou
   ſhalt tread under thy feet.
14 I will deliver him, for hee
   on mee his love hath ſet:
Becauſe that he hath knowne my **Name**,
   I will him ſet on high.
15 Vpon mee he ſhall call in prayʻr,
   and anſwer him will I:
I will be with him when he is
   in troubleſome diſtreſſe,
& I to him will honour give,
   when I ſhall him releaſe.
16 With dayes of long continuance
   Iʻle give to him his fill:
& alſo my ſalvation
   declare to him I will.
     Pſalme 92.
  A pſalme or ſong for the
    Sabbath day.
IT is a good thing to give thanks
   Iehovah thee unto:
unto thy Name prayſes to ſing,
   o thou moſt high alſo.
2 Thy loving kindenes to ſhew forth
     Y 2   with-

within the morning light:
also thy truth, & faithfullnes,
to shew forth every night.

3 Vpon a ten string'd instrument,
and Psaltery upon:
upon the solemne sounding Harp,
a meditation.

4 For through thy work, o Lord, thou hast
mee caused to rejoyce:
and in the workings of thy hands
I will triumph with voyce.

5 O Lord, how mighty are thy works:
thy thoughts are very deepe.

6 The bruitish knows not; nor the foole
this in his heart doth keepe.

7 When as the wicked doe sprirg up
ev'n like the grasse unto,
& all that work iniquity
when as they flourish do:
It's that they then may be destroy'd
to perpetuity.

8 But thou Iehovah dost abide
for evermore most high.

9 For loe, thy foes, for loe, o Lord,
thy foes they perish shall:
the workers of iniquity
they shall be scattred all.

(2)

10 But like the Vnicornes my horne
thou shalt exalt on high:
& with fresh oyle in mine old age

annoynted

annoynted be fhall I.

11 Alfo mine eye fhall fee my wifh
    upon mine enemyes:
mine eare fhall heare of wicked ones,
    that up againft me rife.

12 Like to the Palme tree flourifh fhall
    he that is righteous:
like to a Ceadar he fhall grow
    that is in Lebanus.

13 They that within Iehovahs houfe
    are planted *ftedfaftly*:
within the Courts of our God they
    fhall flourifh *pleafantly*,

14 Their fruit they fhall in their old age
    continue forth to bring:
they fhall be fat, yea likewife they
    fhall ftill be flourifhing:

15 To fhew that upright is the Lord:
    my refuge ftrong is hee,
alfo that there is not in him
    any iniquitee.

Pfalme 93.

THe Lord reigns, cloth'd with majefty:
    God cloath'd with ftrength, doth gird
himfelfe: the world fo ftablifht is,
    that it cannot be ftir'd.

2 Thy throne is ftablifhed of old:

3   from aye thou art. Their voyce
the flouds lift up, Lord, flouds lift up,
    the flouds lift up their noyfe.

4 The Lord on high then waters noyfe

Y 3

more

more ftrong then waves of fea:
5 Thy words moft fure: Lord,holines
becomes thine houfe for aye.

Pfalme 94

O LORD God, unto whom there doe
revenges appertaine:
o God, to whom vengeance belongs,
clearly fhine forth againe.

2 Exalt thy felfe, o thou that art
Iudge of the earth throughout:
render a recompence unto
all thofe that are fo ftout.

3 Iehovah, o how long fhall they
that doe walk wickedly?
how long fhall thofe that wicked are
rejoyce triumphingly?

4 How long fhall thofe men utter forth
& fpeake things that hard bee?
& fhall all fuch thus boaft themfelves
that work iniquitee?

5 Lord, they thy folk in pieces break:
& heritage oppreis.

6 They flay the widdow, & ftranger,
& kill the fatherlefs.

7 The Lord they fay, yet fhall not fee:
nor Iacobs God it minde.

8 Learne vulgar Sots: alfo yee fooles
when will yee wifdome finde?

9 Who plants the eare, fhall he not heare?
who formes the eye, not fee?

10 Who heathen fmites, fhall he not check?

mans

mans teacher, knows not hee?

(2)

11 The Lord doth know the thoughts of man,
    that they are very vaine.
12 Bleſt man whom thou correctſt, o Lord;
    & in thy law doſt traine.
13 That thou mayſt give him quiet from
    dayes of adverſity:
  untill the pit be digged for
    ſuch as doe wickedly.
14 Becauſe Iehovah he will not
    his people caſt away,
  neither will hee forſake his owne
    inheritance for aye.
15 But judgement unto righteouſues
    it ſhall returne agen:
  alſo all upright ones in heart
    they ſhall purſue it *then*.
16 Againſt the evill doers, who
    will up for mee ariſe?
  who will ſtand up for mee 'gainſt them
    that work iniquityes?
17 Had not the Lord me helpt: my ſoule
    had neere in ſilence dwel'd.
18 When as I ſayd, my foot ſlips: Lord,
    thy mercy mee upheld.

(3)

19 Amidſt the multitude of thoughts
    of mine within my minde,
  ſtill from thy conſolations
    my ſoule delight doth finde.

20 Shall

20 Shall the throne of iniquity
    have fellowſhip with thee:
which frameth moleſtation
    and that by a decree?

21 They joyntly gathered themſelves,
    together they withſtood
the ſoule of him that righteous is:
    & condemne guiltleſſe blood.

22 But yet Iehovah unto mee
    he is a refuge high:
alſo my God he is the rock
    of my hopefull ſafety.

23 Their miſchief on them he ſhall bring,
    & in their wickedneſs
he ſhall them cut off : yea, the Lord
    our God ſhall them ſuppreſs.

Pſalme 95.

O Come, let us unto the Lord
    ſhout loud with ſinging voyce.
to the rock of our ſaving health
    let us make joyfull noyſe.

2 Before his preſence let us then
    approach with thankſgiving:
alſo let us triumphantly
    with Pſalmes unto him ſing.

3 For the Lord a great God: & great
    King above all gods is.

4 In whoſe hands are deepes of the earth,
    & ſtrength of hills are his

5 The ſea to him doth appertaine,
    alſo he made the ſame:

and

& alfo the drye land is his
  for it his hands did frame.
6 O come, & let us worfhip give,
  & bowing downe adore:
he that our maker is, the Lord
  o let us kneele before.
7 Becaufe he is our God, & wee
  his pafture people are,
& of his hands the fheep: to day
  if yee his voyce will heare,
8 As in the provocation,
  o harden not your heart:
as in day of temptation,
  within the vaft defart.
9 Whē mee your fathers tryde, & pro'vd,
  & my works lookt upon:
10 Fourty yeares long I griev'd was with
  this generation:
And fayd, this people erre in heart:
  my wayes they doe not know.
11 To whom I fware in wrath: if they
  into my reft fhould goe.

Pfalme 96.

SIng to the Lord a new fong: fing
  all th'earth the Lord unto:
2 Sing to Iehovah, bleffe his Name,
  ftill his falvation fhow.
3 To'th heathen his glory, to all
  people his wonders fpread.
4 For great's the Lord, much to be prayf'd,
  above all gods in dread.

Z   5 Becaufe

5 Becauſe vaine Idols are they all
    which heathens Gods doe name:
but yet Iehovah he it is
    that did the heavens frame.

6 Honour & comely majeſty
    abide before his face:
both fortitude & beauty are
    within his holy place.

7 Yee kindreds of the people *all*
    unto the Lord afford,
glory & mightynes alſo
    give yee unto the Lord.

8 The glory due unto his name
    give yee the Lord unto;
offer yee an oblation,
    enter his courts alſo.

(2)

9 In beauty of his holynes
    doe yee the Lord adore:
the univerſall earth *likewiſe*
    in feare ſtand him before.

10 'Mong heathens ſay, Iehovah reigns:
    the world in ſtablenes
ſhall be, unmov'd alſo: he ſhall
    judge folk in righteouſnes.

11 O let the heav'ns *therat* be glad,
    & let the earth rejoyce:
o let the ſea, & it's fullnes
    with roaring make a noyſe.

12 O let the field be full of joye,
    & all things there about:

                                    then

then all the trees that be i'th wood
they joyfully shall shout
13 Before Iehovah, for he comes,
he comes earths judge to bee.
the world with justice, & the folke
judge with his truth shall hee.

Psalme 97

THe Lord doth reigne, the earth
o let heerat rejoyce:
the many Isles with mirth
let them lift up their voyce.

2 About him round
dark clouds there went,
right & judgement
his throne doe found.

3 Before him fire doth goe,
& burnes his foes about.

4 The world was light also
by lightnings he sent out:
the earth it saw
& it trembled.

5 The hills melted
like wax away
At presence of the Lord:
at his presence who is
of all the earth the Lord.

6 That righteousnes of his
the heavens high
they doe forth show:
all folk also
see his glory.

Z 2   7 who

7 Who graven Images
doe ſerve, on them remaine
let dreadfull ſhamefullnes:
& who in Idols vaine
themſelves doe boaſt:
with worſhip bow
to him all you
Gods Angells *hoaſt*.

8 Sion heard, & was glad,
glad Iudahs daughters were,
this cauſe, o Lord, they had,
thy judgements did appeare.

9 For Lord thou high
all earth ſet o're:
all Gods before
in dignity.

10 Yee that doe love the Lord,
the evill hate doe yee;
to his Saints ſoules afford
protection doth hee:
he will for them
freedome command
out of the hand
of wicked men.

11 For men that righteous are
ſurely there is ſowne light:
& gladnes for their ſhare
that are in heart upright.

12 Ioy in the Lord,
yee Iuſt confeſſe;
his holyneſſe

while

while yee record.

Pſalme 9 8.

A Pſalme

A New ſong ſing unto the Lord,
 for wonders he hath done:
his right hand & his holy arme
 him victory hath wonne.

2 Iehovah his ſalvation
 hath made for to be knowne:
his righteouſnes i'th heathens ſight
 hee openly hath ſhowne.

3 To Iſr'ells houſe of his mercy
 & truth hath mindefull been:
the ends of all the earth they have
 our Gods ſalvation ſeene.

4 Vnto Iehovah all the earth,
 make yee a joyfull noyſe:
make yee alſo a cheerfull ſound,
 ſing prayſe, likewiſe rejoyce.

5 With Harp ſing to the Lord; with Harp,
 alſo with a Pſalms voyce.

6 *With* Trumpets, Cornets ſound; before
 the Lord the King rejoyce.

7 The ſea let with her fullnes roare:
 the world, & there who dwell.

8 O let the flouds clap hands: let hills
 rejoyce together well

9 Before the Lord, for he doth come
 to judge the earth: rightly
with juſtice ſhall he judge the world,
 & folk with equity.

Z 3   PSALM

Pfalme 99.

IEHOVAH 'tis that reigns,
    let people be in dread:
    'midst Cherubs he remaines,
    th'earth let itbe moved.
2   Iehovah is
    in Sion great,
    in highnes fet
        he is likewife
    Above all the people.
3   Let them confeffe thy Name
    fo great & terrible:
    for holy is the fame.
4   The King his might
    doth love juftice:
    thou doft ftablifh
        things that be right:
    Iudgement thou doft, alfo
    in Iacob righteoufnes.
5   The Lord our God doe you
    fet up in his highnes,
        & worfhip yee
    his footftoole at:
    by reafon that
        holy is hee.
6   Mofes alfo Aron
    among his Priefts, likewife
    Samuell all thofe among
    that to his name fend cryes:
        called they have
    the Lord upon,

and

and he *alone*
them anſwer gave.

7 He unto them did ſpeake
it'h cloudy pillar: *then*
they kept his records, eke
his ord'nance he gave them.

8 Lord, thou who art
our God didſt heare,
& didſt anſwer
to them impart,
Thou waſt a God pard'ning
them, although thou vengeance
upon their works didſt bring.

9 The Lord our God advance,
& bow yee downe
at's holy hill:
for our God's *ſtill*
the Holy-one.

Pſalme 100.

A Pſalme of prayſe.

MAke yee a joyfull ſounding noyſe
unto Iehovah, all the earth:

2 Serve yee Iehovah with gladnes:
before his preſence come with mirth.

3 Know, that Iehovah he is God,
who hath us formed it is hee,
& not our ſelves: his owne people
& ſheepe of his paſture are wee.

4 Enter into his gates with prayſe,
into his Courts with thankfullnes:
make yee confeſſion unto him,

and

& his name reverently bleſſe.

5 Becauſe Iehovah he is good,
for evermore is his mercy:
& unto generations all
continue doth his verity.

Another of the ſame.

MAke yee a joyfull noyſe unto
Iehovah all the earth:

2 Serve yee Iehovah with gladnes:
 before him come with mirth.

3 Know, that Iehovah he is God,
 not wee our ſelves, but hee
hath made us: his people, & ſheep
 of his paſture are wee.

4 O enter yee into his gates
 with prayſe, & thankfullneſſe
into his Courts: confeſſe to him,
 & his Name doe yee bleſſe.

5 Becauſe Iehovah he is good,
 his bounteous-mercy
is everlaſting: & his truth
 is to eternity.

Pſalme 101.

A pſalme of David.

MErcy & judgement I will ſing,
Lord, I will ſing to thee.

2 I'le wiſely doe in perfect way:
 when wilt thou come to mee?
I will in midſt of my houſe walk
 in my hearts perfectnes:

3 I will not ſet before mine eyes

matter

matter of wickednes:
I hate their worke that turne aſide,
    it ſhall not cleave mee to.
4 Froward in heart from mee ſhall part,
    none evill will I know.
5 I'le cut him off, that ſlaundereth
    his neighbour privily:
I cannot beare the proud in hearr,
    nor him that looketh high.
6 Vpon the faithfull in the land
    mine eyes ſhall be, that they
may dwell with mee: he ſhall mee ſerve
    that walks in perfect way.
7 Hee that a worker is of guile,
    ſhall not in my houſe dwell:
before mine eyes he ſhall not be
    ſetled, that lies doth tell.
8 Yea, all the wicked of the land
    early deſtroy will I:
to cutt off from Gods citty all
    that work iniquity.

Pſalme 102

A prayer of the afflicted when he is over-
whelmed, & poureth out his complaint
before the Lord.

LORD, heare my ſupplication,
    & let my cry come thee unto:
2 I'th day when trouble is on mee,
    thy face hide not away mee fro:
    Thine eare to mee doe thou incline,
    i'th day I cry, ſoone anſwer mee:

3 For as the smoake my dayes consume,
   & like an hearth my bones burnt bee.

4   My heart is smote, & dryde like grasse,
   that I to eate my bread forget:

5 By reason of my groanings voyce
   my bones unto my skin are set.

6   Like Pelican in wildernes,
   like Owle in desart so am I:

7 I watch, & like a sparrow am
   on house top solitarily.

8   Mine enemies daily mee reproach:
   'gainst mee they rage, 'gainst mee they sweare:

9 That I doe ashes eate for bread:
   & mixe my drink with weeping-teare.

10   By reason of thy fervent wrath
   & of thy vehement-disdaine:
   for thou hast high advanced mee,
   & thou hast cast mee downe againe.

(2)

11   My dayes as shaddow that decline:
   & like the withered grasse am I.

12 But thou, Lord, dost abide for aye:
   & thy Name to eternity.

13   Thou wilt arise, & wilt shew forth
   thy tender-mercy on Sion:
   for it is time to favour her,
   yea the set time is now come on.

14   For in her stones thy servants doe
   take pleasure, & her dust pitty.

15 And heathens shall the Lords Name feare.
   & all Kings of th'earth thy glory.

16 when

16   When as the Lord fhall Sion build
hee in his glory fhall appeare.

17   The poor's petition hee'l regard,
& hee will not defpife their pray'r.

18   This fhall in writing be inroll'd
for the fucceeding-after-race:
that people alfo which fhall bee
created, they the Lord may prayfe.

19   For from his Sanctuary high
from heavn's the Lord the earth doth fee:

20 To heare the groanes of prifoners:
to loofe them that deaths children bee.

21   The Lords prayfe in Ierufalem:
his Name in Sion to record.

22 when people are together met,
& Kingdomes for to ferve the Lord.

(3)

23   He weakned hath i'th way my ftrength,
& fhortened my dayes hath hee.

24 I fayd, in middeft of my dayes
my God doe not away take mee:
Thy yeares throughout all ages are.

25 Thou haft the earth's foundation layd
for elder time: & heavens bee
the work which thine owre hands have made.

26   They perifh fhall, but thou fhalt ftand:
they all as garments fhall decay:
& as a wearing-veftiment
thou fhalt the change, & chang'd are they.

27   But thou art ev'n the fame: thy yeares
they never fhall confumed bee.

23 Thy servants children shall abide,
    & their seed stablisht before thee.
        Psalme 103.
     A psalme of David.

O Thou my soule, Iehovah blesse,
    & all things that in me
most inward are, in humblenes
    his Holy-Name blesse ye

2 The Lord blesse in humility,
    o thou my soule: also
put not out of thy memory
    all's bounties, thee unto.

3 For hee it is who pardoneth
    all thine iniquityes:
he it is also who healeth
    all thine infirmityes.

4 Who thy life from destruction
    redeems: who crowneth thee
with his tender compassion
    & kinde benignitee.

5 Who with good things abundantlee
    doth satissie thy mouth:
so that like as the Eagles bee
    renewed is thy youth.

6 The Lord doth judgement & justice
    for all oppressed ones.

7 To Moses shew'd those wayes of his:
    his acts to Isr'ells sonnes.
        (2)

8 The Lord is mercifull also
    hee's very gracious:

                  and

and unto anger hee is flow,
in mercy plenteous.

9 Contention he will not maintaine
to perpetuity:
nor he his anger will retaine
unto eternity.

10 According to our fins *likewife*
to us hee hath not done:
nor hath he our iniquityes
rewarded us upon.

11 Becaufe even as the heavens are
in height the earth above:
fo toward them that doe him feare
confirmed is his love.

12 Like as the Eaft & *Weft* they are
farre in their diftances:
he hath remov'd away fo far
from us our trefpaffes.

13 A fathers pitty like unto,
which he his fonnes doth beare:
like pitty doth Iehovah fhow
to them that doe him feare.

14 For he doth know this frame of ours:
he minds that duft wee bee.

15 Mans dayes are like the graffe: like flowrs
in field, fo flourifheth bee.

16 For over it the winde doth paffe,
& it away doth goe;
alfo the place wheras it was
noe longer fhall it know.

Aa 3   17 But

17 But yet Gods mercy ever is,
    shall be,& aye hath been
  to them that feare him; and's justice
    unto childrens children.
18 To such as keepe his covenant,
    that doe in minde up lay
  the charge of his commandement
    that it they may obey.
19 The Lord hath in the heavens hye
    established his throne:
  and over all his Royallty
    doth beare dominion.
20 O yee his Angells that excell
    in strength, blesse yee the Lord,
  that doe his word, that harken well
    unto the voyce of 's word.
21 All yee that are the Lords armies,
    o blesse Iehovah *still*:
  & all yee ministers of his,
    his pleasure that fullfill.
22 Yea, all his works in places all
    of his dominion,
  blesse yee Iehovah: o my Soul,
    Iehovah blesse *alone*.

Psalme 104.

THe Lord blesse,o my Soule, o Lord
    my God, exceedingly
great art thou: thou with honour art
    cloath'd & with majesty.
2 Who dost thy selfe with light, as *if*

it were a garment cover:
who like unto a curtaine doſt
the heavens ſtretch all over.

3 Who of his chambers layes the beames
ith waters, & hee makes
the cloudes his Charrets, & his way
on wings of winde hee takes.

4 His Angells Spirits, his miniſters
who makes a fiery flame.

5 who earths foundations layd, that ne're
ſhould be remov'd the ſame.

6 Thou with the deep (as with a robe)
didſt cover the *dry land*:
above the places mountainous
the waters they did ſtand.

7 When as that thou rebukedſt them
away then fled they faſt:
they alſo at thy thunders voyce
with ſpeed away doe haſt.

8 Vp by the mountaines they aſcend:
downe by the valleys go,
the place which thou didſt found for them
untill they come unto.

9 Thou haſt to them a bound prefixt
which they may not paſſe over:
ſo that they might noe more returne
againe the earth to cover.

(2)

10 who ſprings into the valleys ſends,
which run among the hills.

11 whence all beaſts of the field have drink:

wilde

wilde affes drink their fills.

12 Heavns fowles dwell by them, which do fing
among the fprigs with mirth.

13 Hee waters from his lofts the hills:
thy works fruit fill the earth.

14 For beafts hee makes the graffe to grow,
herbs alfo for mans good:
that hee may bring out of the earth
what may be for their food:

15 Wine alfo that mans heart may glad,
& oyle their face to bright:
and bread which to the heart of man
may it fupply with might.

16 Gods trees are fappy: his planted
Cedars of Lebanon:

17 Where birds doe neft: as for the Storke,
Firres are her manfion.

18 The wilde Goates refuge are the hills:
rocks Conies doe inclofe.

19 The Moone hee hath for feafons fet,
the Sun his fetting knows.

(3)

20 Thou makeft darknes, & 'tis night:
when wood beafts creep out all.

21 After their prey young Lions roare:
from God for food they call.

22 The Sun doth rife, then in their dennes
they couch, when gone afide.

23 Man to his work & labour goes,
untill the ev'ning-tide.

24 O Lord, how many are thy works.

all of them thou haſt wrought
in wiſdome: with thy plenteous ſtore
the earth is fully fraught.

25 So is this great & ſpatious ſea,
wherin things creeping bee
beyond all number: beaſts of ſmall
& of great quantitee.

26 There goe the ſhips: Leviathan,
therin thou madſt to play.

27 Theſe all wayt on thee, that their meate
in their time give thou may.

23 They gather what thou giveſt them:
thy hand thou op'neſt wide,
& they with ſuch things as are good
are fully ſatiſſyde.

29 Thou hia'ſt thy face, they troubled are,
their breath thou tak'ſt away,
then doe they dye: alſo returne
unto their duſt doe they.

30 They are created, when thou makſt
thy ſpirit forth to go:
thou of the earth doſt make the face
to be renew'd alſo.

(4)
31 The glory of Iehovah ſhall
for evermore indure:
in his owne works Iehovah ſhall
joyfully take pleaſure.

32 The earth doth tremble, when that hee
upon the ſame doth look,
the mountaines he doth touch, likewiſe

Bb

they

they therupon do fmoak.

34 Full fweet my meditation
concerning him fhall be:
fo that I in Iehovah will
rejoyce *exceedinglee.*

35 *Let* finners be confum'd from th'earth,
& wicked be no more:
bleffe thou Iehovah, o my foule,
prayfe yee the Lord *therefore.*

Pfalme 105.

O Prayfe the Lord, call on his Name.
mong people fhew his facts.

2 Sing unto him, fing pfalmes to him:
talk of all's wondrous acts.

3 Let their hearts joy, that feek the Lord:
boaft in his Holy-Name.

4 The Lord feek, & his ftrengh: his face
alwayes feek yee *the fame.*

5 Thofe admirable works that hee
hath done remember you:
his wonders, & the judgements which
doe from his mouth *iffue.*

6 O yee his fervant Abrahams feed:
fonnes of chofe Iacob yee.

7 He is the Lord our God: in all
the earth his judgements bee.

8 His Covenant for evermore,
and his comanded word,
a thoufand generations to
he doth in minde record,

9 Which he with Abraham made, and's oath

10   to Iſack. Made it faſt,
   a law to Iacob: & Iſr‘ell
    a Cov‘nant aye to laſt.

(2)

11 He ſayd, I‘le give thee Canans land:
    by lot, heirs to be there.
12 When few, yea very few in count
    and ſtrangers in‘t they were;
13 When they did from one nation
    unto another paſs:
   when from one Kingdome their goings
    to other people was,
14 He ſuffred none to doe them wrong:
    Kings checkt he for their ſake:
15 Touch not mine oynted ones; none ill
    unto my Prophets make.
16 He cal‘d for Famine on the land,
    all ſtaffe of bread brake hee.
17 Before them ſent a man: Ioſeph
    ſold for a ſlave to bee.
18 Whoſe feet they did with fetters hurt:
    in yr‘n his ſoule did lye.
19 Vntill the time that his word came:
    the Lords word did him trye.
20 The King the peoples Ruler ſent,
    looſ‘d him & let him go.
21 He made him Lord of all his houſe:
    of all‘s wealth ruler too:
22 At‘s will to binde his Peers: & teach
23   his Ancients ſkill. Then came
   Iſr‘ell to Egypt: & Iacob

         B b 2   ſojourn‘d

PSALM C v.

sojourn'd i'th land of Ham.
24 Hee much increaft his folk: & made
them ftronger then their foe,
25 Their heart he turn'd his folk to hate
to's fervants craft to fhow.

(3)

25 Mofes his fervant he did fend:
& Aaron whom he chofe.
27 His fignes & wonders them amongft,
they in Hams land difclofe.
28 Hee darknes fent, & made it dark:
nor did they's word gain-fay.
29 Hee turn'd their waters into bloud:
& he their fifh did flay.
30 Great ftore of Frogs their land brought forth
in chambers of their Kings.
31 He fpake,there came mixt fwarmes,& lice
in all their coafts *he brings.*
32 He gave them haile for raine: & in
their land fires flame did make.
33 And fmote their Vines & their Figtrees:
& their coaft-trees he brake.
34 He fpake, & then the Locufts came:
& Caterpillars, fuch
the number of them was as none
could reckon up how much,
35 And ate all their lands herbs: & did
fruit of their ground devoure.
36 All firft borne in their land he fmote:
the chief of all their powre.

37 with

(4)

37 With silver also & with gold
   he them from thence did bring:
   & among all their tribes there was
   not any one weak ling.

38 Egypt was glad when out they went:
   for on them fell their dread.

39 A cloud for cov'ring, & a fire
   to light the night he spred.

40 They askt, & he brought quailes: did them
   with heav'ns bread satisfy,

41 He op't the rock and waters flow'd:
   flouds ran in places dry.

42 For on his holy promise, hee
   and's servant Abraham thought.

43 With joye his people, and with songs
   forth he his chosen brought.

44 He of the heathen people did
   the land on them bestow:
   the labour of the people they
   inherited also:

45 To this intent that his statutes
   they might observe *alwayes*:
   also that they his lawes might keepe.
   doe yee Iehovah prayse.

Psalme 106.

PRayse yee the Lord, o to the Lord
   give thanks, for good is hee:
for his mercy continued is
   to perpetuitee.

2 Who can the Lords strong acts forth tell?

Bb 3   or

or all his prayse display?

3 Blest they that judgement keep: & who
   doth righteousnes alway.

4 With favour of thy people, Lord,
   doe thou remember mee:
and mee with that salvation
   visit which is of thee:

5 To see thy chosens good, to joy
   in gladnes of thy nation:
that with thine owne inheritance
   I might have exultation.

6 As our fore-fathers so have wee
   sinned erroniously:
wee practis'd have iniquity,
   wee have done wickedly.

(2)

7 Our fathers did not understand
   thy wonders in Egypt,
nor was thy mercyes multitude
   in their remembrance kept:
But at the sea at the red sea

8   vext him. Yet for his owne
Names sake he sav'd them: that he might
   his mighty powre make knowne.

9 The red sea also he rebuk't,
   and dryed up it was:
so that as through the wildernes,
   through depths he made them pass.

10 And from the hand of him that did
   them hate, he set them free:
and them redeemed from his hand

                        that

that was their enemee.

11 The waters covered their foes:
of them there was left none.

12 They did believe his word; they sang
his prayses therupon.

(3)

13 They soone forgot his words; nor would
they for his counsell stay:

14 But much i'th wildernes did lust;
i'th desart God tryde they.

15 And he their suite them gave; but sent
leannes their soule into.

16 They envi'd Moses in the camp,
Aaron Gods Saint also.

17 The opned earth, Dathan devour'd;
and hid Abirams troup.

18 And fire was kindled in their rout:
flame burnt the wicked up.

19 In *H*oreb made a calfe; also
molt image worshipt they.

20 They chang'd their glory to be like,
an oxe that eateth hay.

21 They God forgot their saviour; which
in Egipt did great acts:

22 *W*orks wondrous in the land of *H*am:
by th'red sea dreadfull facts.

23 And sayd he would them waste; had not
Moses stood (whom he chose)
fore him i'th breach, to turne his wrath,
lest that hee should waste *those*.

24 Yet

(4)

24 Yet they despis'd the pleasant land:
  nor did believe his word:

25 But murmur'd in their tents: the voyce
  they heard not of the Lord.

26 To make them fall i'th desart then,
  'gainst them he lift his hands.

27 'Mongst nations eke to fell their seed,
  and scatter them i'th lands.

28 And to Baal-Peor they joyn'd themselves:
  ate offrings of the dead.

29 Their works his wrath did thus provoake:
  the plague amongst them spread.

30 Then Phineas rose, & judgement did:
  and so the plague did stay.

31 Which justice to him counted was:
  to age and age for aye.

(5)

32 At th'waters of contention
  they angred him also:
 so that with Moses for their sakes,
  it *very* ill did go:

33 Because his spirit they provoakt:
  with's lips to speake rashly.

34 The nations as the Lord them charg'd,
  they stroyd not utterly:

35 But were amongst the Heathen mixt,
  and learn'd their works to do:

36 And did their Idols serve; which them
  became a snare unto.

37 Yea, unto divills, they their sonnes

and

and daughters offered.

38 And guiltlesse bloud, bloud of their sons
    & of their daughters shed,
  Whom unto Canans Idols they
    offred in sacrifice :
  the land with bloud abundantly
    polluted was likewise.

39 Thus with the works were they defylde
    which they themselves had done:
  and they did goe a whoring with
    inventions of their owne:

(6)

40 Therefore against his folk the wrath
    was kindled of the *L*ord:
  so that he the inheritance
    which was his owne abhorr'd.

41 And he gave them to heathens hand;
    their haters their lords were.

42 Their foes thral'd them; under their hand
    made them the yoake to beare.

43 Oft he deliverd them; but they
    provoakt him bitterly
  with their counsell, & were brought low
    for their iniquity.

44 Yet, he regarded their distresse;
    when he did heare their plaint.

45 And he did to remembrance call
    for them his Covenant:
  And in his many mercyes did

46 repent. And made them bee
  pitty'd of all that led them forth

Cc

into

into captivitee.

47 Save us, o Lord our God, & us
from heathens gath'ring rayſe
to give thanks to thy Holy-Name:
to triumph in thy prayſe.

48 The Lord the God of Iſraell
from aye to aye bleſt bee:
and let all people ſay Amen.
o prayſe Iehovah yee.

THE
FIFT   BOOKE

Pſalme 107.

O Give yee thanks unto the Lord,
   becauſe that good is hee:
becauſe his loving kindenes laſts
   to perpetuitee.

2 So let the Lords redeem'd ſay: whom
   hee freed from th'enemies hands:

3 And gathred them from Eaſt, & Weſt,
   from South, & Northerne lands.

4 I'th deſart, in a deſart way
   they wandred: no towne finde,

5 to dwell in. Hungry & thirſty:
   their ſoule within them pinde.

6 Then did they to Iehovah cry
   when they were in diſtreſſe:
who did them ſet at liberty

out

out of their anguishes.

7 In such a way that was most right
   he led them forth also:
that to a citty which they might
   inhabit they might go.

8 O that men would Iehovah prayse
   for his great goodnes *then*:
& for his workings wonderfull
   unto the sonnes of men.

9 Because that he the longing soule
   doth throughly satisfy:
the hungry soule he also fills
   with good abundantly.

(2)

10 Such as in darknes' and within
   the shade of death abide;
who are in sore affliction,
   also in yron tyde:

11 By reason that against the words
   of God they did rebell;
also of him that is most high
   contemned the counsell.

12 Therefore with molestation
   hee did bring downe their heart:
downe did they fall, & none their was
   could help to them impart.

13 Then did they to Iehovah cry
   when they were in distress:
who did them set at liberty
   out of their anguishes.

14 He did them out of darknes bring,

also

also deaths shade from under:
as for the bands that they were in
he did them break asunder.

15 O that men would Iehovah prayse
for his great goodnes *then*:
and for his workings wonderfull
unto the sonnes of men.

15 For he hath all to shivers broke
the gates that were of brasse:
& hee asunder cut each barre
that made of yron was.

(3)

17 For their transgressions & their sins,
fooles doe affliction beare.

18 All kinde of meate their soule abhorres:
to deaths gate they draw neare.

19 Then did they to Iehovah cry
when they were in distress:
who did them set at liberty
out of their anguishes.

20 He, sent his word, & therewithall
healing to them he gave:
from out of their destructions
he did them also save.

21 O that men would Iehovah prayse,
for his great goodnes *then*:
& for his workings wonderfull
unto the sons of men.

22 And sacrifices sacrifice
let them of thanksgiving:
& while his works they doe declare

let

let them for gladnes sing.

(4)

23 They that goe downe to'th sea in ships:
   their busines there to doo
24 in waters great. The Lords work see,
   it'h deep his wonders too.
25 Because that he the stormy winde
   commandeth to arise:
which lifteth up the waves therof,
26 They mount up to the skyes:
   Downe goe they to the depths againe,
   their soule with ill doth quaile.
27 They reele,& stagger,drunkard like,
   and all their witt doth faile.
28 Then did they to Iehovah cry
   when they were in distress:
and therupon he bringeth them
   out of their anguishes.
29 Hee makes the storme a calme: so that
   the waves therof are still.
30 Their rest then glads them; he them bring
   to'th hav'n which they did will.
31 O that men would Iehovah prayse
   for his great goodnes *then*:
& for his workings wonderfull
   unto the sons of men.
32 Also within the peoples Church
   him let them highly rayse:
where Elders are assembled,there
   him also let them prayse.

33 Hee

(5)

33 He rivers to a defart turnes,
    to drought the fpringing well:
34 A fruitfull foyle to barrennes;
    for their fin there that dwell.
35 The defart to a poole he turnes;
    and dry ground to a fpring.
36 Seates there the hungry; who prepare
    their towne of habiting,
37 Vineyards there alfo for to plant,
    alfo to fow the field;
which may unto them fruitfull things
    of much revenue yield.
33 Alfo he blesfeth them, fo that
    they greatly are increaft:
and for to be diminifhed
    he fuffers not their beaft.
39 Againe they are diminifhed
    & they are brought downe low,
by reafon of their presfing-ftreights,
    afflicttion & forrow.

(6)

40 On Princes he contempt doth powre;
    and caufeth them to ftray
i'th folitary wildernes,
    wherin there is no way.
41 Yet hee out of afflicttion
    doth make the poore to rife:
& like as if it were a flock
    doth make him families.
42 The righteous fhall it behold,

and

and be fhall joyfull bee:
in filence ftop her mouth alfo
fhall all iniquitee.

43 Who fo is wife, & who fo will
thefe things attentive learne:
the loving-kindenes of the Lord
they clearely fhall difcerne.

Pfalme 108.

A fong or pfalme of David.

O GOD, my heart's fixt, I'le fing;prayfe
fing ev'n with my glory.

2 Awake thou Pfaltery & Harp;
I will awake early.

3 O thou Iehovah, thee will I
the people prayfe among:
within the midft of nations
thee will I prayfe with fong.

4 For o're the heav'ns thy mercys great;
to'th fkyes thy truth doth mount.

5 Or'e heav'ns o God, be lift, all earth
let thy glory furmount:

6 That thy beloved people may
be fet at libertee:
with thy right hand falvation give,
& doe thou anfwer mee.

(2)

7 God hath in his *owne* holines
fpoken, rejoyce I fhall:
of Shechem I'le divifion make;
& mete out Succoths vale.

8 Mine Gilead, mine Manaffeh is,

and

& Ephraim alſo hee
is of my head the ſtrength: Iudah
ſhall my law-giver bee.

9 Moab my waſh-pot, I will caſt
over Edom my ſhoo:
I'le make a ſhout triumphantly
over Philiſtia too.

10 Who is it that will bring me to
the citty fortifyde?
who is it that into Edom
will be to mee a guide?

11 Wilt not thou doe this thing, o God,
who didſt us caſt thee fro?
& likewiſe wilt not thou o God,
forth with our armies go?

12 From trouble give us help; for vaine
is mans ſalvation.

13 Through God wee ſhall do valiantly;
for hee'l our foes tread downe.

Pſalme 109.

To the chief muſician, a pſalme
of David.

GOD of my prayſe, hold not thy peace,
For mouth of the wicked,
& mouth of the deceitfull are
againſt mee opened:
Gainſt mee they ſpeake with lying tongue.

3   And compaſſe mee about
with words of hate; & mee againſt
without a cauſe they fought.

4 They for my love mine enemies are:

but

but I my prayer make.

5 And ill for good rewarded mee
    & hate for my loves sake.

6 A wicked person over him
    doe thou make for to sit,
also at his right hand doe thou
    let Satan stand at it.

7 When he is judged, let him then
    condemned be therin:
and let the prayr that hee doth make.
    be turned into sin.

8 Few let his dayes bee: & let his
    office another take.

9 His children let be fatherlesse,
    and's wife a widow make.

10 Let's children still be vagabonds,
    begge they their bread also:
out of their places desolate
    let them a seeking go.

(2)

11 Yea, let th'extortioner catch all
    that doth to him pertaine:
and let the stranger spoyle what he
    did by his labour gaine.

12 Let there not any bee that may
    mercy to him expresse:
nor any one that favour may
    his children fatherlesse.

13 The ishue also let thou be
    cut off that from him came:
it'h following generation

Dd   out

out blotted be his name.

14 Remembred with the Lord be his
    fathers iniquitee:
and of his mother never let
    the sin out blotted bee.

15 Before Iehovah let them bee
    continually put:
that from out of the earth he may
    the mem'ry of them cut.

16 Because that he remembred not
    compassion to impart,
but did pursue the needy poore:
    to slay the broke in heart.

(3)

17 As he did cursing love, so let
    cursing unto him come:
as he did not in blessing joy,
    so be it far him from.

18 With cursing like a robe as hee
    cloath'd him: so let it go
like water to his bowels, and
    like oyle his bones into.

19 Garment like let it to him be,
    himselfe for to aray:
and for a girdle, wherewith hee
    may gird himselfe alway.

20 Thus let mine adversaryes bee
    rewarded from the Lord:
also of them against my soule
    that speak an evil word.

21 But

21 But God the Lord, for thy Names sake,
   o doe thou well for mee:
 because thy mercy it is good,
   o doe thou set mee free.

22 For poore & needy I: in mee
   my heart's wounded also.

23 Like falling shade I passe: I 'me tost
   Locust like to & fro.

24 Through fasts my knees are weak: my flesh
   it's fatnes doth forsake.

25 And I am their reproach: they look
   at mee, their heads they shake.

26 Help mee, o Lord my God: after
   thy mercy save thou mee:

27 That they may know this is thy hand:
   Lord that i'ts done by thee.

28 Let them curse, but o doe thou blesse;
   when as that they arise
 let them be shamed, thy servant
   let him rejoyce likewise.

29 Mine adversaryes o let them
   with shame be cloath'd upon:
 & themselves cloath as with a cloak
   with their confusion.

30 I'le to Iehovah with my mouth
   give thanks exceedingly:
 yea him among the multitude
   with prayse I'le glorify.

31 For hee shall stand at right hand of
   the poore & needy one:

Dd 2   from

from those that doe condemne his soule
to give salvation.

Psalme 110.

A psalme of David.

THe Lord did say unto my Lord,
   sit thou at my right hand:
till I thine enemies make a stoole
   wheron thy feet may stand.

2 The Lord the rod shall of thy strength
   send from out of Sion:
in middest of thine enemies
   have thou dominion.

3 Willing thy folk in thy dayes powre,
   in holy beautyes bee:
from mornings womb; thou hast the dew
   of thy youth unto thee.

4 Iehovah sware, nor will repent,
   thou art a Priest for aye:
after the order that I of
   Melchizedeck did say.

5 The Lord who is at thy right hand.
   wounding shall strike through Kings
in that same day wherin that hee
   his indignation brings.

6 Hee shall among the heathen judge,
   and fill with bodies dead
great places, & o're many lands
   he shall strike through the head.

7 Out of the torrent he shall drink
   i'th way *hee passeth by*:
because of this therefore hee shall

lift

lift up his head on hye.

Pfalme III.

PRayfe yee the Lord: with my whole heart
Iehovah prayfe will I:
    i'th private meetings of th'upright,
    and publicke affembly.
2 Great are the Lords works: fought of all
    that in them have pleafure.
3 Comely & glorious is his work:
    aye doth his juftice dure.
4 To be remembred he hath made
    his doings merveilous:
    full of compaffion is the Lord
    as well as gracious.
5 Meate hath hee given unto them
    that fearers of him bee:
    he evermore his covenant
    doth keepe in memoree:
6 The power of his works hee did
    unto his people fhow:
    that he the heathens heritage
    upon them might beftow.

(2)

7 Both verity & judgement are
    the working of his hands:
    yea very faithfull alfo are
    each one of his commands.
8 For ever & for evermore
    they ftand in ftablenes:
    yea they are done in verity
    alfo in uprightnes.

Dd 3   9 Redemption

9 Redemption to his folk he ſent,
    that covenant of his
for aye he hath ordaind: holy
    and reverend his Name is.
10 Of wiſdome the begining is
    Iehovahs feare : all they
that doe his will have prudence good:
    his prayſe indures for aye.

Pſalme 112.

PRayſe yee the *Lord*. bleſt is the man
    that doth Iehovah feare,
that doth in his commandements
    his ſpirit greatly cheare.
2 The *very* mighty upon earth
    ſhall be that are his ſeed:
they alſo ſhall be bleſſed that
    from th' upright doe proceed.
3 And there ſhall be within his houſe
    both wealth & much rich ſtore:
his righteouſnes it alſo doth
    indure for evermore.
4 In midſt of darknes there doth light
    to upright ones ariſe:
both gracious, & pittyfull,
    righteous he is likewiſe.

(2)

5 A good man hee doth favour ſhow
    & ready is to lend:
and with deſcretion his affayres
    he carryes to an end.
6 That man ſhall not aſſuredly

for ever moved bee:
the righteous man he shall be had
 in lasting memoree.

7 By evill tydings that he heares
he shall not be afrayd:
his trust he putting in the Lord,
 his heart is firmly stayd.

8 His heart is sure established,
 feare shall not him surprise,
untill he see what hee desires
 upon his enemies.

9 He hath disperst, hath giv'n to poore:
 his justice constantly
indureth: & his horne shall be
 with honour lifted hye.

10 The wicked shall see, & be griev'd,
 gnash with his teeth shall hee
and melt away: and their desire
 shall faile that wicked bee.

Psalme 113.

THe Lord prayse yee, prayse yee the Lord
 his servants Gods Name prayse.

2 O blessed be Iehovahs Name,
 from henceforth & alwayes.

3 From rising to the setting sun:
 the Lords Name's to be praysd.

4 The Lord all nations is above:
 o're heav'ns his glory raysd

5 Who is like to, the Lord our God?
 who upon earth doth dwell.

6 Who humble doth himselfe to view,

in heav'n, in earth as well.
7 The needy from the duſt he lifts:
the poore lifts from the dung.
8 That hee with princes may him ſet:
his peoples Peeres among.
9 The barren woman he doth make
to keepe houſe, & to bee
a joyfull mother of children:
wherefore the Lord prayſe yee.

Pſalme 114.

VVHen Iſr'ell did depart
th'Egyptians from among,
and Iacobs houſe from a people
that were of a ſtrange tongue:
2 Iudah his holy place:
Iſrell's dominion was.
3 The ſea it ſaw, & fled: Iordane
was forced back to paſs.
4 The mountaines they did leap
upwards like unto rams:
the litle hills alſo they did
leap up like unto lambs.
5 Thou ſea what made thee flye?
thou Iordane, back to go?
6 Yee mountaines that yee ſkipt like rams:
like lambs yee hills alſo?
7 Earth at Gods preſence dread;
at Iacobs Gods preſence:
8 The rock who turnes to waters lake:
ſprings he from flint ſends thence.

Pſalme

Pſalme 115

NOt to us, not unto us, Lord,
 but glory to thy Name afford:
  for thy mercy, for thy truths ſake.
2 The heathen wherefore ſhould they ſay:
where is their God now gone away?
3 But heavn's our God his ſeat doth make:
Hee hath done whatſoe're he would.
4 Their Idols are ſilver & gold:
  the handy work of men they were.
5 Mouths have they, ſpeachleſſe yet they bee:
eyes have they, but they doe not ſee.
6 Eares have they but they doe not heare:
Noſes have they, but doe not ſmell.
7 Hands have they, but cannot handell,
  feet have they but they doe not go:
And through their throat they never ſpake.
8 Like them are they, that doe them make:
  & all that truſt in them are ſo.
9 Truſt in the Lord o Iſraell,
he is their help, their ſhield as well.
10 O Arons houſe the Lord truſt yee:
Hee is their help, & hee their ſhield.
11 Who feare the Lord, truſt to him yield:
  their help alſo their ſhield is hee.
    (2)
12 The Lord hath mindefull been of us,
he'le bleſſe us, he'le bleſſe Iſr'ells houſe:
  bleſſing he'le Arons houſe afford.
13 He'le bleſſe Gods fearers: great & ſmall.
14 You & your ſons, the Lord much ſhall
    E e   increaſe

15   increase still. You blest of the Lord
16 which heav'n & earth made. Heav'ns heav'ns
the Lords: but th'earth mens sons gives hee. (bee
17   The Lords prayse dead doe not afford:
Nor any that to silence bow.
18 But wee will blesse the Lord both now
    and ever henceforth. prayse the Lord.

Psalme 116.

I Love the Lord, because he doth
    my voice & prayer heare.
2 And in my dayes will call, because
    he bow'd to mee his eare.
3 The pangs of death on ev'ry side
    about beset mee round:
the paines of hell 'gate hold on mee,
    distresse & griefe I found.
4 Vpon *Iehovahs* Name therefore
    I called, *& did say*,
deliver thou my soule, o Lord,
    I doe thee humbly pray.
5 Gracious the Lord & just, our God
    is mercifull also.
6 The Lord the simple keeps: & hee
    sav'd mee when I was low.
7 O thou my soule doe thou returne
    unto thy quiet rest:
because the Lord to thee himselfe
    hath bounteously exprest.
8 For thou hast freed my soule from death,
    mine eyes from teares, from fall
9 my feet. Before the Lord i'th land

of

of living walk I shall.

(2)

10 I did believe, therefore I spake:
afflicted much was I.

11 That every man a lyar is
I did say hastily.

12 What shall I render to the Lord,
to mee for's benefits all.

13 I'le take the cup of saving health
& on the Lords Name call.

14 In presence now of all his folk,
I'le pay the Lord my vowes.

15 Of his Saints, in Iehovahs sight
the death is pretious.

16 I am thy servant, truly Lord
thine owne servant am I:
I am the son of thy hand-maide,
my bands thou didst untye.

17 Of thanksgiving the sacrifice
offer to thee I will:
Iehovahs Name I earnestly
will call upon it still.

18 Vnto Iehovah I will pay
the vowes were made by mee,
now in the presence of all them
that his owne people bee.

19 Within the Courts of the Lords house,
ev'n in the midst of thee
o thou *citty* Ierusalem:
o prayse Iehovah yee.

Psalme 117.

AL nations, prayſe the Lord; him prayſe
all people. For his mercies bee
great toward us: alſo alwayes
the Lords truth laſts. the Lord prayſe yee
Annther of the ſame.

AL nations, prayſe the Lord; all folk
prayſe him. For his mercee
is great to us; & the Lords truth
aye laſts. the Lord prayſe yee.

Pſalme 118.

O Give yee thanks unto the Lord,
becauſe that good is hee;
becauſe his loving kindenes laſts
to perpetuitee.

2 For ever that his mercie laſts
let Iſraell now ſay.

3 Let Arons houſe now ſay, that his
mercie indures for aye.

4 Likewiſe let them now ſay, who of
Iehovah fearers bee;
his loving kindenes that it laſts
to perpetuitee.

5 I did lift up my voice to God
from out of ſtreitnes great;
the Lord mee anſwerd, & mee plac't
in an inlarged ſeat.

6 The Lord's for mee, I will not feare
what man can doe to mee.

7 Iehovah takes my part with them
that of mee helpers bee:
Therefore upon them that mee hate

my

my wishes see shall I.

8 'Tis better to trust in the Lord:
   then on man to rely.

(2)

9 'Tis better to trust on the Lord:
   then trust in Princes put.

10 All nations compast mee, but them
   in Gods Name I'le off cut.

11 They compast mee about, yea they
   mee compassed about:
 but in Iehovahs Name I will
   them utterly root out.

12 They compast mee like Bees, are quencht
   like as of thornes the flame:
 but I will utterly destroy
   them in Iehovahs Name.

13 Thou didst thrust sore to make mee fall:
   the Lord yet helped mee.

14 The Lord my fortitude & song:
   & saving health is hee.

15 The tabernacles of the just
   the voice of joye afford
 & of salvation: strongly works
   the right hand of the Lord.

16 The right hand of Iehovah is
   exalted up on hye:
 the right hand of Iehovah is
   a working valiantly.

(3)

17 I shall not dye, but live: & tell
   what things the Lord worketh.

Ee 3   18 The

18 The Lord did forely chaften mee:
     but gave mee not to death.
19 O fet wide open unto mee
     the gates of righteoufnes:
   I will goe into them, & will
     Iehovahs praife confefs.
20 This fame Iehovahs gate at which
     the juft fhall enter in.
21 I'le praife thee, for thou haft mee heard,
     and haft my fafety bin.
22 The ftone which builders did refufe
     head corner ftone now lyes.
23 This is the doing of the Lord:
     it's wondrous in our eyes,

(4)

24 This is the very day the which
     Iehovah hee hath made:
   wee will exceedingly rejoyce,
     & in it will be glad.
25 Iehovah I doe thee befeech,
     falvation now afford:
   I humbly thee intreat, now fend
     profperity, o Lord.
26 Hee that comes in Iehovahs Name
     o let him bleffed bee:
   out of Iehovahs houfe to you
     a blefling with doe wee.
27 God he Iehovah is, and hee
     light unto us affords:
   the facrifices binde unto
     the altars hornes with cords.

                              Thou

28 Thou art my God, & I'le thee prayse,
   my God I'le set thee hye.
29 O prayse the Lord, for he is good,
   and aye lasts his mercy.

Psalme 119.

א   (1)   Aleph

ALL-blest are men upright of way:
   walk in Iehovahs law who do.

2 Blest such as doe his records keepe:
   with their whole heart him seek also.

3   And that work no iniquitie:
   but in his wayes doe walke *indeed*.

4 Thou hast giv'n charge, with diligence
   unto thy precepts to give heed.

5   Ah that to keepe thy statutes:so
   my wayes addressed were by thee.

6 When I respect thy precepts all,
   then shall I not ashamed bee.

7   Whē I thy righteous judgements learne
   with hearts uprig.tnes I'le thee prayse.

8 Forsake thou mee r ot utterly:
   I will observe thy f.atute-wayes.

ב   (2)   Beth

9 By what may ʿ young man cleanse his way?
   by heeding it as thy word guides.

10 With my whole heart thee have I sought:
   thy lawes let mee not goe besides.

11   I in my heart thy word have hid:
   that I might not against thee sin.

12 Thou o Iehovah, blessed art:
   thine owne statutes instruct mee in.

13 All

13 All the juſt judgements of thy mouth
   declared with my lips have I.

14 I in thy teſtimonyes way
   joy more then in all rich plenty.

15   In thy precepts I'le meditate:
   and have reſpect unto thy wayes.

16 My ſelfe I'le ſolace in thy lawes:
   and not forget what thy word *ſayes*.

     ג   (3)   Gimel

17   Confer this grace thy ſervant to,
   that I may live thy word to keep.

18 Vnveile mine eyes, that I may ſee
   out of thy law the wonders *deep*.

19   I am a ſtranger in the earth:
   do not thy precepts from me hide.

20 My ſoule is broken with deſire
   unto thy judgements time & tide.

21   Thou haſt rebuk'd the proud, acurſt
   which doe frō thy commandments ſwerve.

22 Roll off from mee reproach & ſcorne:
   for I thy records doe obſerve.

23   Ev'n Princes ſate & 'gainſt mee ſpake;
   but on thy lawes thy ſervant muſ'd.

24 Thy records alſo are my joyes:
   and for men of my counſell *uſ'd*.

     ד   (4)   Daleth

25   Downe to the duſt my ſoule cleav's faſt:
   o quicken mee after thy word.

26 I ſhow'd my wayes & thou mee heardſt:
   thy ſtatutes learning mee afford.

27   Thy precepts way make mee to know:

ſo I'le muſe on thy wondrous wayes.

28 My ſoule doth melt for heavines:
  according to thy word mee rayſe.

29   The way of lying from mee take:
  and thy law grant mee gracıouſly.

30 The way of truth I choſen have:
  thy judgements *fore mee* layd have I.

31   Thy teſtimonies cleave I to;
  o Lord, on mee ſhame do not caſt.

32 Then ſhall I run thy precepts way,
  when thou mine heart enlarged haſt.

E ⊓ (5) He.
33   Enforme mee Lord, in thy laws path;
  and I will keep it to the end.

34 Skill give mee, & thy law I'le keep:
  yea with my whole heart it attend.

35   Cauſe mee to tread thy precepts path;
  becauſe therin delight I do.

36 Vnto thy records bend my heart;
  & covetouſnes not unto.

37   From vaine ſights turne away mine eyes:
  and in thy way make mee to live.

38 Confirme thy word thy ſervant to,
  who to thy feare himſelfe doth give.

39   My ſlander which I feare remove;
  becauſe thy judgements good they bee.

40 Loe for thy precepts I have lon'gd:
  o in thy juſtice quicken mee.

F ⌐ (6) Vau.
41   Finde mee out let thy mercies Lord:
  thy ſaving health as thou haſt ſayd.

PSALM CXIX.

42 So I my taunters answer shall,
for on thy word my hope is stayd.

43 Nor truths-word quite frō my mouth take:
because thy judgements I attend.

44 So I thy law shall alway keep,
to everlasting without end.

45 And I will walk at libertie,
because I doe thy precepts seek.

46 Nor will I blush, when before Kings
I of thy testimonies speak.

47 In thy commands, which I have lov'd,
also my selfe delight I will.

48 And lift my hands to thy commands
belov'd: & minde thy statutes still.

G (7) Sajin.

49 Good to thy servant make the word,
on which to hope thou didst mee give.

50 This was my comfort in my griefe,
because thy word doth make mee live.

51 The proud have much derided mee:
yet have I not thy law declinde.

52 Thy judgements Lord, that are of old,
I did recall, & comfort finde.

53 Horrour hath taken hold on mee:
for lewd men that thy law forsake.

54 I, in my pilgrimages house,
of thy statutes my songs doe make.

55 By night remembred I thy Name,
o Lord: & I thy law observe.

55 This hath been unto mee, because
I from thy precepts did not swerve.

Hee

H ך (8) Heth.

57 Hee, ev'n the Lord, my portion is,
I said that I would keep thy word.

58 With my whole heart thy face I begg'd:
thy promis'd mercies mee afford.

59 I thought upon my waies, & turn'd
my feet into thy testaments.

60 I hasted, & made no delaies
to keepe with heed thy commandments.

61 The bands of wicked men mee robb'd:
of thy law I am not mindeless.

62 Ile rise at midnight thee to praise;
for judgements of thy righteousnes.

63 Companion am I to all them,
that feare thee, & thy laws doe heed.

64 Thy mercie fills the earth, o Lord:
teach mee the lawes thou hast decreed.

I ט (9) Teth.

65 Iehovah, with thy servant thou
after thy word, right-well hast done.

66 Good taste & knowledge, teach thou mee,
for I believe thy precepts on.

67 Before I was chastis'd, I stray'd:
but I thy word observ'd have now.

68 Thou art good, & art doing good:
thy statutes teach mee, oh doe thou.

69 The proud against mee forg'd a lye:
thy laws I'le keepe with my hearts-might.

70 The heart of them is fat as grease:
but in thy law I doe delight.

71 It's good for mee, I was chastis'd:

Ff 2

that

that so thy statutes learne I should.

72 Better to mee is thy mouths-law,
then thousands of silver & gold.

K' (10) Iod.

73 Know make mee, & I'le learn thy lawes:
thy hands mee formed have, & made.

74 Who feare thee, mee shall see, & joy:
because hope in thy word I had.

75 Thy judgements Lord, I know are just;
& faithfully thou chastnedst mee.

76 As thou hast to thy servant spoke,
now let thy grace my comfort bee.

77 Send mee thy grace, that I may live;
for thy law as my joy I chuse.

78 Shame proud ones, that mee falsly wrong:
but I will in thy precepts muse.

79 Let them that feare thee turne to mee;
and such as have thy records knowne.

80 Let my heart bee in thy lawes sound
that so I shame may suffer none.

L כ (11) Caph.

81 Look for thy word I doe, *when as*
my soule doth faint for help from thee.

82 Mine eies have failed for thy word,
saying, when wilt thou comfort mee?

83 I like a smoake-dride-bottle am;
yet doe I not thy laws forgoe.

84 what are thy servants daies? when wilt
on my pursuers judgement doe?

85 The proud have digged pits for mee,
which doe not unto thy law sute.

All

86 All thy comands are truth: help mee,
   they wrongfully mee perfecute.

87   They nigh had wafted mee on earth,
   but I thy laws did not forfake.

88 To keep the records of thy mouth,
   mee in thy mercie lively make.

M 7   (12)   Lamed.

89 Made faft i'th heavens is thy word,
   o Lord, for ever to endure.

90 From age to age thy faithfullnes:
   thou form'dft the earth, & it ftands-fure.

91   As thou ordain'dft, they ftill abide;
   for all are fervants thee unto.

92 Had not thy law been my delight:
   Then had I perifht in my wo.

93   Thy ftatutes I will ne're forget:
   becaufe by them thou quicknedft mee.

94 Thine owne am I, fave mee, becaufe
   I fought thy precepts ftudiouflee.

95   The wicked watch mee, mee to ftroy:
   but I thy teftimonies minde.

96 Of all perfection, end I fee:
   but very large thy law *I finde.*

N D   (13)   Mem.

97 Now how much doe I love thy law?
   it is my ftudy all the day.

98 Thou mad'ft mee wifer then my foes
   by thy rule: for it's with mee aye.

99   I'me wifer then my teachers all:
   for thy records my ftudy are.

100 I more then ancients underftand;

becaufe

because I kept thy laws with care.

101   From each ill path my feet I stay'd:
that so I might thy word observe.

102 Because thou hast instructed mee,
I did not from thy judgements swerve.

103 How sweet are thy words to my taste?
to my mouth more then honie they.

104 I from thy precepts wisdome learne:
therefore I hate each lying way.

O   (14) Nun.

105 Of my feet is thy word the lamp:
and to my path the shining light.

106 Sworne have I, & will it performe,
that I will keep thy judgements right.

107 I am afflicted very much:
Lord quicken mee after thy word.

108 Accept my mouths free-offrings now:
& mee thy judgements teach o Lord.

109 My soule is alwaies in my hand:
but I have not thy law forgot.

110 The wicked laide for mee a snare:
yet from thy laws I strayed not.

111 Thy recods are mine heritage
for aye: for my hearts joy they bee.

112 I bent my heart still to performe
thy statues to eternitee.

P   (15) Samech.

113 Pursue-I doe with hatred, all
vaine thoughts: but love thy law doe I.

114 My covert & my shield art thou:
I on thy word wait hopefully.

Bee

115 Depart from mee, lewd men, that I
  may keepe my Gods commandements.

116 By thy word stay mee, & I live:
  nor shame mee for my confidence.

117 Susteine mee, & I shall be safe:
  and in thy law still I'le delight.

118 thou tread'st downe all that from thy laws
  doe stray: for false is their deceit.

119 All th'earths lewd ones like drosse thou-
  therefore thy records love I do. (stroyd'st

120 For feare of thee my flesh doth quake:
  I doe thy judgements dread also.

Q y (16) Hajin.

121 Quite to oppressors leave mee not:
  I judgement doe, & righteousnes.

122 thy servants suretie be for good:
  let not the proud ones mee oppress.

123 Mine eyes for thy salvation faile:
  as also for thy righteous word.

124 In mercie with thy servant deale:
  & thy lawes-learning mee afford.

125 I am thy servant, make mee wise,
  thy testimonies for to know.

126 Time for thee Lord it is to work,
  for men thy law doe overthrow.

127 Therefore doe I thy precepts love,
  above gold, yea the finest gold.

128 All false paths hate I: for thy rules
  of all things, are all right, I hold.

R ב (17) Pe.

129 Right-wondrous are thy testimonies:
        there-

therefore my soule keeps them with care.

130 The entrance of thy words gives light:
and makes them wise that simple are.

131 I gape & pant for thy precepts;
because I longed *for the same.*

132 Look on mee, & such grace mee show,
as thou dost them that love thy Name

133 My steps by thy word guide: & let
no wickednes beare rule in mee.

134 From mens oppression mee redeem:
and thy laws-keeper will I bee.

135 Make thy face on thy servant shine:
and mee to learne thy statutes cause.

136 Mine eies run floods of waters downe:
because they doe not keep thy laws.

S   ץ   (18)   Tzade.

137 incerely-just art thou, o Lord,
thy judgements upright are also.

138 Thy testimonies thou commandst
are right, yea, very faithfull too.

139 My zeale consumed mee, because
mine enemies thy words forget.

140 Thy word it is exceeding pure:
therefore thy servant loveth it.

141 Small am I, & contemptible:
yet thy commands forget not I.

142 Thy justice, justice is for aye:
also thy law is verity.

143 Distresse & anguish seas'd on mee:
yet thy commands delights mee give.

144 *Thy records justice lasts for aye:*

also

make thou mee wife, & I fhall live.

T ק (19) Koph.

145   o mee that cry with my whole heart
Lord heare: thy ftatutes keep I will.

146 I unto thee did cry: fave mee,
    & I fhall keep thy records ftill.

147   The dawning I prevent, & cry:
    I for thy word doe hopefull-waite.

148 Mine eyes prevent the night-watches,
    in thy word for to meditate.

149   Lord, of thy mercy heare my voice:
    after thy judgements quicken mee.

150 Who follow mifchiefe, they draw nigh:
    who from thy law afarre off bee.

151   But o Iehovah, thou art neere:
    and all thy precepts verity.

152 I long fince of thy records knew:
    thou laid'ft them for eternity.

V ר (20) Refch.

153   iew mine affliction, & mee free:
    for I thy law doe not forget.

154 Plead thou my caufe, & mee redeem:
    for thy words fake alive mee fet.

155   Salvation from lewd men is far:
    fith they thy laws to finde ne're ftrive.

156 Great are thy bowell- mercies Lord:
    after thy judgements mee revive.

157   Many my foes and hunters are:
    yet I not from thy records fwerve.

158 I faw tranfgreffors, & was griev'd,
    for they thy word doe not obferve.

Gg   See

159   See Lord, that I thy precepts love:
graunt, of thy bounty live I may.

160 Thy word's beginning it is truth:
and all thy right judgements for aye.

W⃝ (21)   Schin.

161   ithout cause Princes mee pursue:
but of thy word my hearts in awe.

162 As one that hath much booty found,
so I rejoyce doe in thy law.

163   Lying I hate, & it abhorre:
but thy law dearly love doe I.

164 Seven times a day I prayse thee, for
the judgements of thine equity.

165   Great peace have they that love thy law:
& such shall finde no stumbling-stone.

166 I hop't for thy salvation, Lord:
and thy commandments I have done.

167   My soule thy testimonies keeps:
and them I love exceedinglee.

168 I keep thy rules & thy records:
for all my waies before thee bee.

Y⃝ (22)   Thau.

169   ield Lord, my cry, t'approach thy face:
as thou hast spoke, mee prudent make.

170 Let my request before thee come:
deliver mee for thy words sake.

171   My lips shall utter forth *thy* prayse:
when thou thy lawes hast learned mee.

172 My tongue shall forth thy word resound:
for all thy precepts justice *bee*.

173 To help mee let thy hand be neere:

for thy commandments chofe have I.

274 I long for thy falvation, Lord:
    and my delights in thy law *ly*.

275   Let my foule live, & fhew thy prayfe:
    help mee alfo thy judgements let.

276 Like loft fheep ftrayd, thy fervant feeke:
    for I thy laws doe not forget

Pfalme 120.

A fong of degrees.

VNto the Lord, in my diftreffe
    I cry'd, & he heard mee.

2 From lying lipps & guilefull tongue,
    o Lord, my foule fet free.

3 What fhall thy falfe tongue give to thee,
    or what on thee confer?

4 Sharp arrows of the mighty ones,
    with coales of juniper.

5 Woe's mee, that I in Mefech doe
    a fojourner remaine:
    that I doe dwell in tents, which doe
    to Kedar appertaine.

6 Long time my foule hath dwelt with him
    that peace doth much abhorre,

7 I am for peace, but when I fpeake,
    they ready are for warre.

Pfalme 121.

A fong of degrees.

I To the hills lift up mine eyes,
    from whence fhall come mine aid.

2 Mine help doth from Iehovah come,
    which heav'n & earth hath made.

Gg 3   3 Hee

3 Hee will not let thy foot be mov'd,
   nor slumber; that thee keeps.
4 Loe hee that keepeth Israell,
   hee slumbreth not, nor sleeps.
5 The Lord thy keeper is, the Lord
   on thy right hand the shade.
6 The Sun by day, nor Moone by night,
   shall thee by stroke *invade.*
7 The Lord will keep the from all ill:
   thy soule hee keeps alway,
8 Thy going out, & thy income,
   the Lord keeps now & aye.

Psalme 122.
A song of degrees.

I Ioy'd in them, that to mee syd
   to the Lords house go wee.
2 Ierusalem, within thy gates,
   our feet shall standing bee.
3 Ierusalem, it builded is
   like unto a citty
   together which compacted is
   within it selfe closely.
4 Whether the tribes, Gods tribes ascend
   unto Isr'ells witnes;
   that they unto Iehovahs Name
   may render thankfullnes.
5 For there the judgements thrones, the thrones
   of Davids house doe sit.
6 O for Ierusalem her peace
   see that yee pray for it:
   Prosper they shall that doe theelove.

7 peace

7   Peace in thy fortreſſes
   o let there be, proſperity
    within thy Pallaces.
8 For my brethren & for my friends,
    I'le now ſpeake peace to thee.
9 I'le for our God Iehovahs houſe,
    ſeek thy felicitee.

Pſalme 123.
A ſong of degrees.

O Thou that ſitteſt in the heav'ns,
   I lift mine eyes to thee.
2 Loe, as the ſervants eyes unto
   hand of their maſters bee:
As maides eyes to her miſtreſſe hand,
   ſo are our eyes unto
the Lord our God, untill that hee
   ſhall mercy to us ſhow.
3 O Lord be mercifull to us,
   mercifull to us bee:
becauſe that filled with contempt
   exceedingly are wee.
4 With ſcorne of thoſe that be at eaſe,
   our ſoule's fill'd very much:
alſo of thoſe that great ones are,
   ev'n with contempt of ſuch.

Pſalme 124.
A ſong of degrees. of David.

H Ad not the Lord been on our ſide,
   may Iſraell now ſay,
2 Had not God been for us, when men
   did riſe againſt us they:

Gg 3   3 The

3 They had then ſwallow'd us alive,
    when their wrath on us burn'd.
4 Then had the waters us o'rewhelmd,
    the ſtreame our ſoule or'e turnd.
5 The proud waters then, on our ſoule
    had paſſed on their way:
6 Bleſt be the Lord, that to their teeth
    did not give us a prey.
7 Our ſoule, as bird, eſcaped is
    out of the fowlers ſnare:
    the ſnare aſunder broken is,
    and wee delivered are.
8 The ſuccour which wee doe injoye,
    is in Iehovahs Name:
    who is the maker of the earth,
    and of the heavens frame.

pſalme 125.

A ſong of degrees.

They that doe in Iehovah truſt
    ſhall as mount Sion bee:
which cannot be remo'vd, but ſhall
    remaine perpetuallee.
2 Like as the mountaines round about
    Ieruſalem doe ſtay:
ſo doth the Lord ſurround his folk,
    from henceforth ev'n for aye.
3 For lewd mens rod on juſt mens lot
    it ſhall not reſting bee:
leſt juſt men ſhould put forth their hand
    unto iniquitee.
4 To thoſe Iehovah, that be good,

gladnes

gladnes to them impart:
as also unto them that are
upright within their heart.
5 But who turne to their crooked wayes,
the Lord shall make them go
with workers of iniquity:
but peace be Ifr'ell to.

psalme 126.
A song of degrees.

VVHen as the Lord return'd againe
Sions captivitee:
at that time unto them that dreame
compared might wee bee.
2 Then was our mouth with laughter fill'd,
with singing then our tongue:
the Lord hath done great things for them
said they, t'heathens among.
3 The Lord hath done great things for us,
wherof wee joyfull bee.
4 As streames in South, doe thou o Lord,
turne our captivitee.
5 Who sow in teares, shall reape in joy.
6 Who doe goe forth,& mourne,
bearing choise seed, shall sure with joye
bringing their sheaves returne.

psalme 127.
A song of degrees for Solomon.

IF God build not the house, vainly
who build it doe take paine:
except the Lord the citty keepe,
the watchman wakes in vaine.

2 I'ts

2 I'ts vaine for you early to rife,
   watch late, to feed upon
   the bread of grief: fo hee gives fleep
   to his beloved one.

3 Loe, the wombes fruit, it's Gods reward
   fonnes are his heritage.

4 As arrows in a ftrong mans hand,
   are fons of youthfull age.

5 O bleffed is the man which hath
   his quiver fill'd with thofe:
they fhall not be afham'd, i'th gate
   when they fpeake with their foes.

Pfalme 128.

A fong of degrees.

BLeffed is every one
   that doth Iehovah feare:
   that walks his wayes along.

2 For thou fhalt eate *with cheare*
   thy hands labour:
   bleft fhalt thou bee,
   it well with thee
   fhall be therefore.

3 Thy wife like fruitfull vine
   fhall be by thine houfe fide:
   the children that be thine
   like olive plants abide
   about thy board.

4 Behold thus bleft
   that man doth reft,
   that feares the Lord.

5 Iehovah fhall thee bleffe

from

from Sion, & shalt see
Ierusalems goodnes
all thy lifes dayes that bee.
6 And shalt view well
thy children then
with their children,
  peace on Isr'ell.

  Psalme 129.
  A song of degrees.

FRom my youth, now may Isr'ell say,
 oft have they mee assaild:
2 They mee assaild oft from my youth,
 yet 'gainst mee nought prevaild.
3 The ploughers plough'd upon my back,
 their furrows long they drew:
4 The righteous Lord the wickeds cords
 he did asunder-hew.
5 Let all that Sion hate be sham'd,
 and turned back together.
6 As grasse on house tops, let them be,
 which ere it's grown, doth wither:
7 Wherof that which might fill his hand
 the mower doth not finde:
nor therewith hee his bosome fills
 that doth the sheaves up binde.
8 Neither doe they that passe by, say,
 Iehovahs blessing bee
on you: you in Iehovahs Name
a blessing wish doe wee.

  Psalme 130.
  A song of degrees.
   H h   psalme

PSALM C xxx, Cxxxi.

LORD, from the depth I cryde to thee.
    My voice Lord, coe thou heare:
unto my supplications voice
    let be attent thine eare.
3 Lord, who should stand? if thou o Lord,
    shouldst mark iniquitee.
4 But with thee there forgivenes is:
    that feared thou maist bee.
5 I for the Lord wayt, my soule wayts:
    & I hope in his word.
6 Then morning watchers watch for morn,
    more my soule for the Lord.
7 In God hope Isr'ell, for mercy
    is with the Lord: with him
8 there's much redemption. From all's sin
    hee Isr'ell will redeem.

Psalme 131.

A song of degrees, of David.

MY heart's not haughty, Lord,
    nor lofty are mine eyes:
in things too great, or high for mee,
    is not mine exercise.
2 Surely my selfe I have
    compos'd, and made to rest,
like as a child that weaned is,
from off his mothers *brest*:
    Im'e like a weaned child.
3 Let Israell then stay
with expectation on the Lord,
    from henceforth and for aye.

Psalme 132.

A song

PSALME Cxxxii.

A song of degrees.

Remember David, Lord,
and all's affliction:
2 How to the Lord he swore, & vow'd
to Iacobs mighty one.
3 Surely I will not goe
my houses tent into:
upon the pallate of my bed,
thither I will not go.
4 I will not verily
give sleep unto mine eyes:
nor will I give to mine eye-lidds
slmber *in any wise,*
5 Vntill that for the Lord
I doe finde out a seate:
a fixed habitation,
for Iacobs God so great.
6 Behould, at Epratah,
there did wee of it heare:
ev'n in the plain-fields of the wood
wee found it *to be there.*
7 Wee'l goe into his tents:
wee'l at his footstoole bow.
8 Arise, Lord, thou into thy rest:
and th'Arke of thy strength *now.*
9 Grant that thy priests may be
cloathed with righteousnes:
o let thy holy ones likewise
shout forth for joyfullnes.
10 Let not for Davids sake   *2 part.*
a servant unto thee,

Hh 2   the

the face of thine annoynted one
   away quite turned bee.
11 The Lord to David sware
    truth, nor will turne from it;
thy bodyes fruit, of them I'le make
   upon thy throne to sit.
12 If thy sons keep my law,
    and covenant, I teach them;
upon thy throne for evermore
   shall sit their children then.
13 Because Iehovah hath
    made choise of *mount* Sion:
he hath desired it to bee
   his habitation.
14 This is my resting place
    to perpetuity:
here will I dwell, and that because
   desired it have I.
15 Blesse her provision
    abundantly I will:
the poore that be in her with bread
   by mee shall have their fill.
16 Her Priests with saving health
    them also I will clad:
her holy ones likewise they shall
   with shouting loud be glad.
17 The horne of David I
    will make to bud forth there:
a candle I prepared have
   for mine annoynted *deare.*
18 His enemies I will

                            with

with fhame apparrell them:
but flourifhing upon himfelfe
fhall be his Diadem:

Pfalme 133.

A fong of degrees, of David.

HOw good and fweet o fee,
i'ts for brethren to dwell
together in unitee:

2   It's like choife oyle *that fell*
the head upon,
that downe did flow
the beard unto,
beard of Aron:
The fkirts of his garment
that unto them went downe;

3   Like Hermons dews defcent,
Sions mountaines upon,
for there to bee
the Lords blefsing,
life aye lafting
commandeth hee.

Annother of the fame.

HOw good it is, o fee,
and how it pleafeth well,
together ev'n in unitee
for brethren foe to dwell:

2   I'ts like the choife oyntment
from head, to'th beard did go,
downe Arons beard: downeward that went
his garments fkirts unto.

3   As Hermons dew, which did

Hh 3   on

on Sions hill defcend:
for there the Lord bleffing doth bid,
ev'n life without an end.

Pfalme 134.

A fong of degrees.

O All yee fervants of the Lord,
behold the Lord bleffe yee;
yee who within Iehovahs houfe
i'th night time ftanding bee.

2 Lift up your hands, and bleffe the Lord,
in's *place* of holines.

3 The Lord that heav'n & earth hath made,
thee out of Sion blefs.

Pfalme 135.

THe Lord praife, praife ye the Lords Name:
the Lords fervants o praife him yee.

2 That in the Lords houfe ftand: *the fame*
i'th Courts of our Gods houfe who bee.

3 The Lord prayfe, for the Lord is good:
for fweet its to his Name to fing.

4 For Iacob to him chofe hath God:
& Ifr'ell for his pretious thing.

5 For that the Lord is great I know:
& over all gods, our Lord keeps.

6 All that he wills, the Lord doth do:
in heav'n, earth, feas, & in all deeps.

7 The vapours he doth them conftraine,
forth from the ends of th'earth to rife;
he maketh lightning for the raine:
the winde brings from his treafuries.

(2)

3   Of Egipt he the firſt borne ſmit:
and that of man, of beaſts alſo.

9   Sent wondrous ſignes midſt thee, Egipt:
on Pharoah, on all's ſervants too.

10   Who ſmote great natiōs, ſlew great Kings:

11   Slew Sihon King of th'Amorites,
Og alſo one of Baſhans kings:
all kingdomes of the Cananites,

12   And gave their land an heritage:
his people Iſr'ells lot to fall.

13   For aye thy Name, Lord, through each age
o Lord, is thy memoriall.

14   For his folks judge, the Lord is hee:
and of his ſervants he'le repent.

15   The heathens Idols ſilver bee,
& gold: mens hands did them invent.

16   Mouths have they, yet they never ſpake:
eyes have they, but they doe not ſee:

17   Eares have they, but no hearing take:
& in their mouth no breathings bee.

18   They that them make, have their likenes:
that truſt in them ſo is each one.

19   The Lord o houſe of Iſr'ell bleſs;
the Lord bleſſe, thou houſe of Aaron.

20   O houſe of Levi, bleſſe the Lord:
who feare the Lord, bleſſe ye the Lord.

21   From Sion bleſſed be the Lord;
who dwells at Salem praiſe the Lord.

Pſalme 136.

pſalme

PSALM CxxxVI.

O Thank the Lord, for hee is good:
for's mercy lasts for aye.

2 Give thanks unto the God of gods:
for's mercy is alway.

3 Give thanks unto the Lord of lords:
for's mercy lasts for aye.

4 To him who only doth great signes:
for's mercy is alway.

5 To him whose wisdome made the heav'ns:
for's mercy &c.

6 Who o're the waters spread the earth:
for's mercy &c.

7 Vnto him that did make great lights:
for's mercy &c.

8 The Sun for ruliug of the day:
for's mercy &c.

9 The Moone and Stars to rule by night:
for's mercy &c.

10 To him who Egipts first-borne smote:
for's mercy &c.

11 And from amongst them Isr'ell brought:
for's mercy &c.

12 With strong hand, & with stretcht-out arme:
for's mercy &c.

13 To him who did the red sea part:
for's mercy &c.

14 And through i'ts midst made Isr'ell goe:
for's mercy &c.

15 But there dround Pharoah & his hoast:
for's mercy &c.

16 His people who through desart led:

for's

for's mercy &c.

17 To him which did fmite mighty Kings:
　　for's mercy &c.
18 And put to flaughter famous Kings:
　　for's mercy &c.
19 Sihon King of the Amorites:
　　for's mercy &c.
20 And Og who was of Bafhan King:
　　for's mercy &c.
21 And gave their land an heritage:
　　for's mercy &c.
22 A lot his fervant Ifraell to:
　　for's mercy &c.
23 In our low ftate who minded us:
　　for's mercy &c.
24 And us redeemed from our foes:
　　for's mercy &c.
25 Who giveth food unto all flefh:
　　for's mercy lafts for ay.
26 Vnto the God of heav'n give thanks:
　　for's mercy is alway.

Pfalme 137.

THe rivers on of Babilon
　　there when wee did fit downe:
yea even then wee mourned, when
　　wee remembred Sion.
2 Our Harps wee did hang it amid,
　　upon the willow tree.
3 Becaufe there they that us away
　　led in captivitee,
Requit'd of us a fong, & thus

I i

a/kt

askt mirth: us waste who laid,
 sing us among a Sions song,
  unto us then they said.
4 The lords song sing can wee? being
5 in strangers land. Then let
loose her skill my right hand, if I
  Ierusalem forget.
6 Let cleave my tongue my pallate on,
  if minde thee doe not I:
if chiefe joyes or'e I prize not more
  Ierusalem my joy.
7 Remember Lord, Edoms sons word,
  unto the ground said they,
it rase, it rase, when as it was
  Ierusalem her day.
8 Blest shall hee bee, that payeth thee,
  daughter of Babilon,
who must be waste: that which thou hast
  rewarded us upon.
9 O happie hee shall surely bee
  that taketh up, that eke
thy little ones against the stones
  doth into pieces breake.

Psalme 138.
A psalme of David.

VVIthall my heart, I'le prayse thee *now:*
 before the gods I'le sing to thee.
2 Toward thine holy Temple bow,
 & praise thy Name for thy mercee,
  & thy truth: for thy word thou hye
or'e all thy Name dost magnify.

3 I$\mathfrak{c}$h

PSALME Cxxxviii.

3   It'h day I cride, thou anſwredſt mee:
with ſtrength thou didſt my ſoule up-beare.

4   Lord, all the earths kings ſhall praiſe thee,
the word when of thy mouth they heare.

5   Yea, they ſhall ſing in the Lords wayes,
for great's Iehovahs glorious prayſe.

6   Albeit that the Lord be hye,
reſpeƈt yet hath he to the low:
but as for them that are lofty,
he them doth at a diſtance know.

7   Though in the midſt I walking bee
of trouble thou wilt quicken mee,
Forth ſhalt thou make thine hand to go
againſt their wrath that doe me hate;
thy right hand ſhall me ſave alſo.

8   The Lord will perfeƈt mine eſtate:
thy mercy Lord, for ever ſtands:
leave not the works of thine owne hands.

Another of the ſame.

VVIthall my heart, I'le thee confeſs:
thee praiſe the gods before.

2 The Temple of thine holines
towards it I'le adore:
Alſo I will confeſſe thy Name,
for thy truth, & mercy:
becauſe thou over all thy Name
thy word doſt magnify.

3 In that ſame day that I did cry,
thou didſt mee anſwer make:
thou ſtrengthnedſt mee with ſtrength, which I
within my ſoule *did take.*

Ii 2   4 O

4 O Lord, when thy mouths words they heare
   all earths Kings shall thee praise.
5 And for the Lords great glory, there
   they shall sing in his wayes.
6 Albeit that the Lord be high,
   yet hee respects the low:
   but as for them that are lofty
   hee them far off doth know.
7 Though I in midst of trouble go,
   thee quickning mee I haue:
   thy hand thou wilt cast on my foe,
   thy right hand shall mee saue.
8 The Lord will perfect it for mee:
   thy mercy ever stands,
   Lord, doe not those forsake that bee
   the works of thine owne hands.

Psalme 139.
To the chief musician, a psalme
of David.

O LORD, thou hast me searcht & knowne.
   Thou knowst my sitting downe,
& mine up-rising: my thought is
   to thee afarre off knowne.
3 Thou knowst my paths, & lying downe,
   & all my wayes knowst well.
4 For loe, each word that's in my tongue,
   Lord, thou canst fully tell.
5 Behinde thou gird'st mee, & before:
   & layst on mee thine hand.
6 Such knowledge is too strange, too high,
   for mee to understand

7 where

7 Where shall I from thy presence go?
  or where from thy face flye?

8 If heav'n I climbe, thou there, loe thou,
  if downe in hell I lye.

9 If I take mornings wings; & dwell
  where utmost sea-coasts bee.

10 Ev'n there thy hand shall mee conduct:
   & thy right hand hold mee.

11 That veryly the darknes shall
   mee cover, if I say:
   then shall the night about mee be
   like to the lightsome day.

12 Yea, darknes hideth not from thee,
   but as the day shines night:
   alike unto thee both these are,
   the darknes & the light.

13 Because that thou possessed hast
   my reines: and covered mee
   within my mothers wombe thou hast.

14 My prayse shall be of thee,
   Because that I am fashioned
   in fearfull wondrous wise:
   & that thy works are merveilous,
   my soule right well descries.

(2)

15 From thee my substance was not hid,
   when made I was closely:
   & when within th'earths lowest parts
   I was wrought curiously.

16 Thine eyes upon my substance yet
   imperfected, did look,

and

& all the members that I have
were written in thy booke,
What dayes they fhould be fafhioned:
none of them yet were come.

17 How pretious are thy thoughts to mee,
o God? how great's their fumme?

18 If I fhould count them, in number
more then the fands they bee:
& at what time I doe awake,
ftill I abide with thee.

19 Affuredly thou wilt o God,
thofe that be wicked flay:
yee that are bloody men, therefore
depart from mee away.

20 Becaufe that they againft thee doe
fpeake wickedly *likewife*:
thy Name they doe take up in vaine
who are thine enemies.

21 Thy haters Lord, doe I not hate?
& am not I with thofe
offended grievoufly that doe
up-rifing thee oppofe?

22 Them I with perfect hatred hate:
I count them as my foes.

23 Search mee o God, & know my heart:
try mee, my thoughts difclofe:

24 And fee if any wicked way
in mee there bee at all:
& mee conduct within the way
that laft for ever fhall.

Palme 140

PSALME CxL.

To the chief mufician, a pfalme
of David,

L ORD, free mee from the evill man:
from violent man fave mee.
2 Whofe hearts thinke mifchief: every day
for war they gathred bee.
3 Their tongues they have made to be fharp
a ferpent like unto :
the poyfon of the Afpe it is
under their lipps *alfo*.   Selah.
4 Keepe mee, Lord, from the wickeds hands,
from violent man mee fave:
my goings who to overthrow
in thought projected have.
5 The proud have hid a fnare for mee,
cords alfo: they a net
have fpred abroad by the way fide:
grins for mee they have fet.   Selah.
6 Vnto Iehovah I did fay,
thou art a God to mee:
Lord, heare the voice of my requefts,
which are for grace to thee.
(2)
7 O God, the Lord, who art the ftay
of my falvation:
my head by thee hath covered been
the day of battell on.
3 Thofe mens defires that wicked are,
Iehovah, doe not grant,
their wicked purpofe furher not,
left they themfelves doe vaunt.

9 As

9 As for the head of them that mee
    doe round about inclose,
  o let the molestation
    of their lips cover those.
10 Let burning coales upon them fall,
    into the fire *likewise*
  let them be cast, into deepe pits,
    that they no more may rise.
11 Let not i'th earth establisht bee
    men of an evill tongue:
  evill shall hunt to overthrow
    the man of violent wrong.
12 The afflicteds cause, the poore mans right,
    I know God will maintaine:
13 Yea, just shall praise thy Name: th'upright
    shall 'fore thy face remaine.

Psalme 141.
A psalme of David.

O GOD, my Lord, on thee I call,
    doe thou make hast to mee:
  and harken thou unto my voice,
    when I cry unto thee.
2 And let my pray'r directed be
    as incense in thy sight:
  and the up-lifting of my hands
    as sacrifice at night.
3 Iehovah, oh that thou would'st set
    a watch my mouth before:
  as also of my lips with care
    o doe thou keepe the dore.
4 Bow not my heart to evill things;

to doe the wicked deed
with wicked workers: & let not
mee of their dainties feed.

5 Let juſt-men ſmite mee, kindenes 'tis;
let him reprove mee eke,
it ſhall be ſuch a pretious oyle,
my head it ſhall not breake:
For yet my pray r's ev'n in their woes.

6 When their judges are caſt
on rocks, then ſhall they heare my words,
for they are ſweet to taſte.

7 Like unto one who on the earth
doth cutt & cleave the wood,
ev'n ſo our bones at the graves mouth
are ſcattered abroad.

8 But unto thee o God, the Lord
directed are mine eyes:
my ſoule o leave not deſtitute,
on thee my hope relyes.

9 O doe thou keepe mee from the ſnare
which they have layd for mee;
& alſo from the grins of thoſe
that work iniquitee.

10 Together into their owne nets
o let the wicked fall:
untill ſuch time that I eſcape
may make from them withall.

Pſalme 142.
Maſchil of David, a prayer when
he was in the cave.

Kk

pſalm

PSALM CxlII.

VNto Iehovah with my voice,
    I did unto him cry:
unto Iehovah with my voice
    my sute for grace made I.

2 I did poure out before his face
    my meditation:
before his face I did declare
    the trouble mee upon.

3 O'rewhelm'd in mee when was my spirit,
    then thou didst know my way:
I'th way I walkt, a snare for mee
    they privily did lay.

4 On my right hand I lookt, & saw,
    but no man would mee know,
all refuge faild mee: for my soule
    none any care did show.

5 Then to thee Lord, I cryde, & sayd,
    my hope thou art *alone*:
& in the land of living ones
    thou art my portion.

6 Because I am brought very low,
    attend unto my cry:
from my pursuers save thou mee,
    which stronger bee then I.

7 That I thy Name may praise, my soule
    from prison oh bring out:
when thou shalt mee reward, the just
    shall compasse mee about.

Psalme 143.
A psalme of David.

psalm

PSALME Cxliii.

LORD, heare my prayr, give eare when I
doe supplicate to thee:
   in thy truth, in thy righteousnes,
    make answer unto mee.

2 And into judgement enter not
    with him that serveth thee;
   for in thy sight no man that lives
    can justified bee.

3 For th'enemie hath pursude my soule,
    my life to'th ground hath throwne:
   & made mee dwell i'th dark like them
    that dead are long agone.

4 Therefore my spirit is overwhelmd
    perplexedly in mee:
   my heart also within mee is
    made desolate to bee.

5 I call to minde the dayes of old,
    I meditation use
   on all thy words: upon the work
    of thy hands I doe muse.

6 I even I doe unto thee
    reach mine out-stretched hands:
   so after thee my soule doth thirst
    as doe the thristy lands.   Selah.

(2)

7 Hast, Lord, heare mee, my spirit doth faile,
    hide not thy face mee fro:
   lest I become like one of them
    that downe to pit doe go.

8 Let mee thy mercy heare i'th morne,
    for I doe on thee stay,

       wherin

wherin that I should walk cause mee
to underſtand the way:
For unto thee I lift my ſoule.
9   O Lord deliver mee
froːn all mine enemies; I doe flye
to hide my ſelfe with thee.
10 Becauſe thou art my God, thy will
oh teach thou mee to doe,
thy ſpirit is good: of uprightnes
lead mee the land into.
11 Iehovah, mee o quicken thou
ev'n for thine owne Names ſake;
And for thy righteouſnes my ſoule
from out of trouble take.
12 Doe thou alſo mine enemies
cut off in thy mercy,
deſtroy them that afflict my ſoule:
for thy ſervant am I.

Pſalme 144.
A pſalme of David.

O Let Iehovah bleſſed be
who is my rock of might,
who doth inſtruct my hands to war,
and my fingers to fight.
2 My goodnes, fortreſſe, my hye towre,
& that doth ſet mee free:
my ſhield, my truſt, which doth ſubdue
my people under mee.
3 Iehovah, what is man, that thou
knowledge of him doſt take?
what is the ſon of man, that thou

acount

account of him doſt make?

4 Man's like to vanity: his dayes
   paſſe like a ſhade away.

5 Lord, bow the heav'ns, come downe & touch
   the mounts & ſmoake ſhall they.

6 Lightning caſt forth, & ſcatter them:
   thine arrows ſhoot, them rout.

7 Thine hand o ſend thou from above,
   doe thou redeeme mee out:
   And rid mee from the waters great:
   from hand of ſtrangers brood:

8 Whoſe mouth ſpeaks lyes, their right hand is
   a right hand of falſehood.

(2)

9 O God, new ſongs I'le ſing to thee:
   upon the Pſaltery,
   and on ten ſtringed inſtrument
   to thee ſing praiſe will I.

10 It's hee that giveth unto Kings
   ſafety victorious:
   his ſervant David he doth ſave
   from ſword pernitious.

11 Rid mee from hand of ſtrange children,
   whoſe mouth ſpeakes vanity:
   & their right hand a right hand is
   of lying falſity:

12 That like as plants which are growne up
   in youth may be our ſons;
   our daughters pallace like may be
   polliſht as corner ſtones:

13 Our garners full, affording ſtore

Kk 3

of

of every sort of meates;
   our cattell bringing thousands forth,
   ten thousands in our streets:
14 Strong let our oxen bee to work,
   that breaking in none bee
   nor going out: that so our streets
   may from complaints bee free.
15 O blessed shall the people be
   whose state is such as this:
   o blessed shall the people be,
   whose God Iehovah is.

Psalme 145.

Davids psalme of praise.

MY God, o King, I'le thee extoll:
   & blesse thy Name for aye.
2 For ever will I praise thy Name;
   and blesse thee every day.
3 Great is the Lord, most worthy praise:
   his greatnes search can none.
4 Age unto age shall praise thy works:
   & thy great acts make knowne.
5 I of thy glorious honour will
   speake of thy majesty;
   & of the operations
   by thee done wondrously.
6 Also men of thy mighty works
   shall speake which dreadfull are:
   also concerning thy greatnes,
   it I will forth declare:
7 Thy great goodnesses memory
   they largely shall expres:

and

and they shall with a shouting voice
    sing of thy righteousnes.

8 The Lord is gracious, & hee is
    full of compassion:
slow unto anger, & full of
    commiseration.

9 The Lord is good to all: or'e all   *part* (2)
    his works his mercies bee.

10 All thy works shall praise thee, o Lord:
    & thy Saints shall blesse thee,

11 They'le of thy kingdomes glory speake:
    and talk of thy powre *hye*;

12 To make mens sons his great acts know:
    his kingdomes majesty.

13 Thy Kingdome is a kingdome aye:
    & thy reigne lasts alwayes.

14 The Lord doth hold up all that fall:
    and all downe-bow'd ones rayse.

15 All eyes wayt on thee, & their meat
    thou dost in season bring.

16 Opnest thy hand, & the desire
    fill'st of each living thing.

17 In all his wayes the Lord is just:
    & holy in's works all.

18 Hee's neere to all that call on him:
    in truth that on him call.

19 Hee satisfy will the desire
    of those that doe him feare:
Hee will be safety unto them,
    and when they cry he'le heare.

20 The Lord preserves each one of them

                that

that *lovers of* him bee:
but whoſoever wicked are
aboliſh them doth hee.

21 My mouth the prayſes of the Lord
by ſpeaking ſhall expreſs:
alſo all fleſh his holy Name
for evermore ſhall bleſs.

Pſalme 146.

THe Lord praiſe: praiſe(my ſoule) the Lord.
So long as I doe live
I'le praiſe the Lord; while that I am,
praiſe to my God I'le give.

3 Truſt not in Princes; nor mans ſon
who can no ſuccour ſend.

4 His breath goe's forth, to's earth he turnes,
his thoughts that day doe end.

5 Happie is hee that hath the God
of Iacob for his ayd:
whoſe expectation is upon
Iehovah his God ſtayd.

6 Which heav'n, earth, ſea, all in them made:
truth keeps for evermore:

7 Which for th'oppreſſed judgement doth,
gives to the hungry ſtore,

8 The Lord doth looſe the priſoners.
the Lord ope's eyes of blinde,
the Lord doth raiſe the bowed downe;
the Lord to'th juſt is kinde.

9 The Lord ſaves ſtangers, & relievs
the orphan, & widow:
but hee of them that wicked are

the

the way doth overthrow·

10 The Lord shall reigne for evermore,
    thy God, o Sion, hee
to generations all shall reigne:
    o prayse Iehovah yee.

Psalme 147.

PRayse yee the Lord, for it
    is good praises to sing,
to our God for it's sweet,
    praise is a comely thing.

2   Ierusalem
the Lord up-reares,
outcasts gathers
    of Isre'll *them.*

3 The broke in heart he heales:
    & up their wounds doth binde.

4 The stars by number tells:
    hee calls them all by kinde.

5   Our Lord great is,
& of great might,
yea infinite
    his knowledge 'tis.

6 The Lord sets up the low:
    wicked to ground doth fling.

7 Sing thanks the Lord unto
    on Harp, our Gods praise sing.

8   Who clouds the skyes,
to earth gives raines:
who on mountaines
    makes grasse to rise.

9 Beasts, hee & ravens young

when

when as they cry feeds then.

10 Ioyes not in horses strong:
nor in the leggs of men.

11   The Lord doth place
his pleasure where
men doe him feare,
    & hope on's grace.

12 Ierusalem, God praise:
Sion thy God confess:

13 For thy gates barres he stayes:
in thee thy sons doth bless.

14   Peace maketh hee
in borders thine:
with wheat so fine
    hee filleth thee.

15 On earth sends his decree:
swiftly his word doth pass.

16 Gives snow like wool, spreds hee
his hoare frost ashes as.

17   His yce doth cast
like morsels to:
'fore his cold who
    can stand stedfast?

18 His word sends, & them thaws:
makes winde blow, water flows.

19 His word, Iacob; his laws,
& judgements Isr'ell shows.

20   Hee hath so done
no nation to,
judgements also
    they have not knowne.
    Hallelujah,

PSALME Cxlviii.

Pſalme 148. Hallelujah.

FRom heav'n o praiſe the Lord:
   him praiſe the heights within.
2 All's Angells praiſe afford,
   all's Armies praiſe yee him.
3   O give him praiſe
  Sun & Moone *bright*:
  all Stars of light,
    o give him praiſe.
4 Yee heav'ns of heav'ns him praiſe:
  or'e heav'ns yee waters *cleare*.
5 The Lords Name let them praiſe:
  for hee ſpake, made they were.
6   Them ſtabliſht hee
  for ever & aye:
  nor ſhall away
    his madē decree.
7 Praiſe God from th'earth *below*:
  yee dragons & each deepe.
8 Fire & haile, miſt & ſnow:
  whirl-windes his word which keepe.
9   Mountaines, alſo
  you hills all yee:
  each fruitfull tree,
    all Cedars too.
10 Beaſts alſo all cattell:
  things creeping, foules that flye.
11 Earths kings, & all people:
  princes, earths judges *hye*:
    doe all the ſame.
12 Young men & maids:

Ll 2   old

old men & babes.

13   Praise the Lords Name,
For his Name's hye only:
his glory o're earth & heav'n.

14 His folks horne he lifts hye
the praise of all's Saints, ev'n
     the sons who bee
of Israell,
his neere people,
     the Lord praise yee.

Psalme 149.

PRaise yee the Lord: unto the Lord
  doe yee sing a new song:
& in the congregation
  his praise the Saints among.

2 Let Israell now joyfull bee
  in him who him hath made:
children of Sion in their King
  o let them be full glad.

3 O let them with *melodious* flute
  his Name give praise unto:
let them sing praises unto him
  with Timbrell, Harp also.

4 Because Iehovah in his folk
  doth pleasure greatly take:
the meek hee with salvation
  ev'n beautifull will make.

5 Let them the gracious Saints that be
  most gloriously rejoyce:
& as they lye upon their beds
  lift up their singing voyce.

6 let

6 Let their mouths have Gods praise: their hand
    a two edg'd sword also:
7 On heathen vengeance, on the folk
    punishment for to do:
8 Their kings with chaines, with yron bolts
    also their peers to binde:
9 To doe on them the judgement writ:
    all's Saints this honour finde.
              Hallelujah.

Psalme 150.

PRaise yee the Lord, praise God
   in's place of holines:
  o praise him in the firmament
    of his great mightines.
2   O praise him for his acts
    that be magnificent:
  & praise yee him according to
    his greatnes excellent.
3   With Trumpet praise yee him
    that gives a sound so hye:
  & doe yee praise him with the Harp,
    & sounding Psalterye.
4   With Timbrell & with Flute
    praise unto him give yee:
  with Organs, & string'd instruments
    prais'd by you let him bee.
5   Vpon the loude Cymballs
    unto him give yee praise:
  upon the Cimballs praise yee him
    which hye their sound doe raise.

PSALM CI.

6 Let every thing to which
the Lord doth breath afford
the praises of the Lord set forth:
o doe yee praise the Lord.

FINIS

An admonition to the Reader.

THe verses of these psalmes may be reduced to
six kindes, the first wherof may be sung in very neere fourty common tunes; as they are collected, out of our chief musicians, by *Tho. Ravers-
croft.*

The second kinde may be sung in three tunes as
Pf. 25. 50. & 67. in our english psalm books.

The third. may be sung indifferently, as *pf.* the 51.
100. & ten cōmandements, in our english psalme
books. which three tunes aforesaid, comprehend
almost all this whole book of psalmes, as being
tunes most familiar to us.

The fourth. as *pf.* 148. of which there are but a-
bout five.

The fift. as *pf.* 112. or the *Pater noster,* of which
there are but two. *viz.* 8 5. & 158.

The sixt. as *pf.* 113. of which but one, *viz.* 115.

Faults escaped in printing.

Escaped.	Right
psalme 9. vers 9. oprest.	opprest.
v. 10. knowes.	know.
ps. 18. n. 29. the.	thee.
n. 31. 3 part wanting.	3 part.
ps. 29. n. 13, let thou- kept back.	kept back o let.
ps. 31 n. 8. the Lord.	thine hand.
ps. 143. n. 6. Jenen I.	moreover I.

The rest, which have escaped through over-
sight, you may amend, as you finde
them obvious.